LIST OF CONTENTS

LIST OF ILLUSTRATIONS

CHALLENGES TO AUTHORITY:
FICTION AND FILM IN CONTEMPORARY SPAIN

ROBIN W. FIDDIAN AND PETER W. EVANS

CHALLENGES TO AUTHORITY: FICTION AND FILM IN CONTEMPORARY SPAIN

TAMESIS BOOKS LIMITED
LONDON

Colección Támesis
SERIE A - MONOGRAFIAS, CXXIX

DISTRIBUTORS:

Spain:
Editorial Castalia,
Zurbano, 39,
28010 Madrid

United States and Canada:
Longwood Publishing Group,
27 South Main Street,
Wolfeboro, New Hampshire 03894, U.S.A.

Great Britain and rest of the world:
Grant and Cutler Ltd.,
55-57 Great Marlborough Street,
London W1V 2AY

ISBN.: 84-599-2248-0
Depósito Legal: M-2073-1988.
Printed in Spain by Unigraf, S.A. Móstoles, Madrid.

for
TAMESIS BOOKS LIMITED
LONDON

PREFACE

We gratefully acknowledge receipt of grants from the Carnegie Trust for the Universities of Scotland and the University of Newcastle upon Tyne (Sponsorship Committee for Publications), which helped to finance the publication of this book.

We should like to thank the Museo Lázaro Galdiano and the Museo del Prado in Madrid for allowing us to reproduce paintings by Gisbert and Goya. Permission to use stills from Viridiana, Stress es tres, tres and Carmen was granted by Contemporary Films, Elías Querejeta Productions and Curzon Film Distributors Ltd.

The following individuals helped us in various ways: Maggi Hurt of Tyneside Cinema provided information about Arsène Lupin; Lee Fontanella of the University of Texas at Austin identified the location of Gisbert's painting; John Hopewell and Carmen Méndez shared their specialist knowledge of Spanish cinema with us; Sr. José Manuel Caballero Bonald and Doña Carmen Balcells provided factual and bibliographical information; and Professor John Varey of Tamesis Books gave generous advice and encouragement.

Finally, our thanks are due to the staff and students of the Department of Spanish and Latin American Studies of the University of Newcastle upon Tyne for lively discussion and support, and to the Secretary Susan Davidson, for typing parts of the book.

ROBIN W. FIDDIAN,
PETER W. EVANS

The University of Newcastle upon Tyne

IX

INTRODUCTION

This study examines the work of five contemporary Spanish novelists and film directors from a comparative perspective which highlights the interrelationships between film and fiction in Spain in the years since the end of the Civil War. Though not the first book to investigate the connections between Spanish literature and the cinema, it nevertheless differs in crucial respects from other approaches to the subject which have varied markedly in their aims and methodology. In a pioneering study C. B. Morris has documented numerous thematic and stylistic similarities in the films, paintings and poetry of leading figures of the 1920s and 30s.[1] Elsewhere Robert Havard has considered Luis Buñuel's creative re-working of a classic Galdós text in an essay which may serve as a model for the study of recent adaptations for Radio Televisión Española of novels like Camilo José Cela's *La colmena* (directed by Mario Camús in 1982), Miguel Delibes' *Los santos inocentes* (also by Camús, in 1984), and Luis Martín Santos' *Tiempo de silencio* (adapted to the screen in 1985).[2] In another vein Román Gubern has discussed the indebtedness of many film-makers to the tradition of the modern novel with its rich store of narrative devices adaptable to film,[3] while Alan Spiegel's account of the impact of cinematic form on the novel over the last hundred years demonstrates that the interaction between verbal and visual forms of expression in the arts has been reciprocal.[4] These various comparative exercises have two principal features in common: one is a legitimate concern with poetics, i. e. with manifestly important questions of form, genre, influence, and the like; the other is a certain narrowness of perspective which excludes from consideration the relation of those questions to wider contexts of politics, sociology, ideology and history. Our project is directly concerned with the relations between history and art in mid-twentieth-century Spain.

---

[1] CYRIL BRIAN MORRIS, *This Loving Darkness* (Oxford, 1980).

[2] ROBERT HAVARD, «The Seventh Art of Luis Buñuel: "Tristana" and the Rites of Freedom», *Quinquereme,* V, 1 (1982), 56-74.

[3] ROMÁN GUBERN, «El cine en el panorama de la narrativa moderna», in *Cine contemporáneo* (Barcelona, 1973), pp. 23-28.

[4] ALAN SPIEGEL, *Fiction and the Camera Eye. Visual Consciousness in Film and the Modern Novel* (Charlottesville, Virginia, 1976).

In the case studies presented here we consider some of the ways in which Spanish literary and film texts of recent decades have mediated a collective response to economic, social, political and cultural change.

Our analysis focusses on three novels: *Dos días de setiembre* by José Manuel Caballero Bonald (published in 1962), *Tiempo de silencio* by Luis Martín Santos (1962), and *Si te dicen que caí* by Juan Marsé (1973); and three films: *Viridiana* by Luis Buñuel (1961), *Stress es tres, tres* (1968) and *Carmen* (1982), both by Carlos Saura. All are texts which are tied inseparably to the world of historical experience in the dual respects of their systematic treatment of contemporary historical themes and the often controversial circumstances of their composition and publication. Taken together, they reproduce a broad range of temporal settings which include the years of the Civil War and its consequences of poverty and repression, in Andalusia, for example (viz. *Dos días de setiembre*), and of armed resistance, in Catalonia (viz. *Si te dicen que caí*); the late 40s in Madrid before the limited effects of American financial aid were felt in Spanish society (viz. *Tiempo de silencio*); the late 50s and early 60s, when the momentum of economic development and social change accelerated dramatically in Spain (viz. *Dos días de setiembre* and *Viridiana*); the volatile years of the mid- and late 60s (depicted in Saura's *Stress es tres, tres*); and the early 80s, when Spain faced a set of social and political issues (illustrated in *Carmen*) quite distinct from those of the previous decade.

As historians like Ramón Tamames and Paul Preston have observed, the historical process of Spain since the end of the Civil War reveals an overall pattern of development which coincides in the main with the transition from one decade to another. So, it is possible to perceive four clearly delimited stages in the country's economic history between 1939 and 1982, with significant points of articulation in the years 1951, 1962 and 1973. Spain's domestic political history as mapped out by the radical reorganisation of government ministries in July 1951 and July 1962, the assassination of Admiral Carrero Blanco and his replacement as Prime Minister by Arias Navarro in December 1973, and the victory of Felipe González's Socialists in the democratic elections of October 1982, illustrates the same trend, as does a particularly important set of relations between the State and the Church which underwent major transformations in 1953 (when the régime signed a new Concordat with the Vatican), 1961-63 (upon the publication of two encyclicals by Pope John XXIII), and 1971 (when the Joint Assembly of Bishops and Priests issued a communiqué which was sternly critical of some of the policies of the Franco régime).[5]

---

[5] NORMAN COOPER surveys relations between the Church and the Franco State in «The Church: from Crusade to Christianity», in *Spain in Crisis. The Evolution of the Franco Régime*, ed. PAUL PRESTON (Hassocks, Sussex, 1976), pp. 48-81.

This sketchy outline of some general trends in recent Spanish history confirms the practical value of the conventional historiographic tool of analysis-by-decade. At the same time, it draws attention in a more detailed way to certain crucial dates and conjunctures which may be regarded as turning points in contemporary Spanish affairs. In our view, such points of reference provide a useful framework for the texts discussed here, allowing us to perceive them as events embedded in a highly complex field of historical and cultural forces. One such conjuncture may be identified in the years 1955-57. This brief period saw the breakdown of the economic system of autarky which had been instituted in the 1940s and was now hopelessly incompatible with the needs of Spanish society; the eruption of industrial disputes throughout Navarre, the Basque Country, Catalonia, and Madrid; and, in the university sector, multiple disturbances which forced the government to declare a state of emergency and to dismiss two liberalising ministers responsible for university affairs. It was against this background of unrest that there began to appear a significant wave of films and novels committed to the exploration of contemporary social themes. Titles such as *Muerte de un ciclista* (1955) and *Calle mayor* (1956), both directed by Juan Antonio Bardem, *El Jarama* (1955) by Rafael Sánchez Ferlosio, and, to a greater extent, *El circo* (1957) by Juan Goytisolo, exemplified a new social realist mode of expression which was deeply rooted in the historical moment. As José Manuel Caballero Bonald was to remark some 15 years later, «Nuestro realismo fue más bien el degradado afluente de una tradición urgentemente aclimatada a una concreta coyuntura social».[6]

Coming shortly after these critical years, the period 1959-62 represented an even more dramatic conjuncture for the government and people of Spain. In the socio-economic sphere, the Stabilization Plan of 1959 provoked a short-term recession which resulted in emigration on a massive scale (the highest ever total of emigrants leaving Spain was registered in 1961); in internal affairs, the period was marked by continuing industrial unrest in Asturias, and renewed student agitation in Madrid and Barcelona which led —once more— to the declaration of a state of emergency and a major ministerial reshuffle in the summer of 1962, just a few weeks after delegates of the main Spanish opposition parties had met in the historic «contubernio de Munich»; in the cultural sphere, Luis Buñuel returned to Spain from exile in Mexico to make *Viridiana,* and the new Minister of Information and Tourism, Manuel Fraga Iribarne, introduced a more relaxed attitude to the implementation of the strict standards of censorship inherited from his predecessor, Arias Salgado, who had presided over that ministry since 1951. No less than three of the titles selected for study here date from this critical

[6] See FEDERICO CAMPBELL, «José Manuel Caballero Bonald o la penetración del satanismo», in *Infame Turba* (Barcelona, 1971), p. 313.

3

moment when, as Isaac Montero remarks, «La totalidad de la vida española se encuentra abocada a un cambio y urge tomar conciencia de ello». [7]

1968-73 were years of sustained crisis. Divisive debates about the legalising of political associations took place between 1967 and 1969 against a backcloth of severe economic difficulties, open rebellion by the student population in April 1968, and a state of emergency imposed in January 1969. The Matesa scandal broke in July 1969 and forced General Franco to effect what one commentator has termed «el más radical cambio de gobierno hasta entonces realizado»; [8] in the opinion of another, the Matesa affair was nothing less than «el núcleo de la degradación del franquismo». [9] *ETA militar's* assassination of Admiral Carrero Blanco in December 1973 crowned this period of instability of which Saura's *Stress es tres, tres* may be seen as a portent. An archetypal late-sixties text, *Stress* makes a brief and dismissive reference to the second Development Plan for 1968-71 which is announced in a newspaper cutting read by Teresa (Geraldine Chaplin) near the beginning of the film. *Si te dicen que caí* also belongs to this period. The official ban in the autumn of 1973 on the publication of this novel by Juan Marsé points up forcefully the internal contradictions of a régime unable, because of entrenched and anachronistic attitudes, to adjust its policies in line with developments in social and cultural conditions. [10]

The pivotal points of the decade following General Franco's death on 20 November 1975 may not, perhaps, be identified yet with the same degree of certainty as those of the previous thirty-five years. However, if we postulate a period of stability between 1975 and 1980 when consensus politics prevailed in Spain (witness the harmonious outcome of the General Election of 1977, the political success of the Moncloa Pact in October of that year, the approval of the Constitution in the autumn of 1978, and the satisfactory conduct of a further round of elections in 1979), then we have a standard against which to measure subsequent developments such as those which occurred in 1981. The events of January and February of that year —primarily, the resignation of the architect of the transition, Adolfo Suárez, and the spectacular armed occupation of the Cortes by a group of *guardias civiles* led by Lieutenant Colonel Tejero— and, from July on, the hostile reaction in some quarters to controversial proposals for legalising civil divorce which were approved by the Cortes but subsequently obstructed and

---

[7] ISAAC MONTERO, «La novela española de 1955 hasta hoy. Una crisis entre dos exaltaciones antagónicas», *Triunfo*, 507 (17 June 1972), Extra II, p. 88.
[8] See RAMÓN TAMAMES, *La República. La Era de Franco* (Madrid, 1973), p. 529.
[9] See RICARDO DE LA CIERVA, *Historia del Franquismo. Aislamiento, transformación, agonía (1945-1975)* (Barcelona, 1978), p. 308.
[10] SAMUEL AMELL provides some interesting information about the banning of *Si te dicen que caí*, in *La narrativa de Juan Marsé* (Madrid, 1984), pp. 107-09. See also «Entrevista con Juan Marsé, autor de *Si te dicen que caí*, última novela secuestrada», *El Noticiero Universal*, 2 November 1976, p. 15.

4

left unresolved some four years later,[11] mark out 1981 as a year that was crucial for the fortunes of democracy in post-Franco Spain. The historic victory of the Partido Socialista Obrero Español in the General Election of October 1982 consolidated the strength of Spanish democracy, but only after the King and his ministers had neutralised the threat of further military interference in public affairs. Our final text, *Carmen* (1982), is in many respects a reflection of this climate of rapid social change and an oblique comment on the state of the country's institutions at this particular time.

Grounded in precise historical circumstances and encompassing a wide range of temporal reference, our six texts are thus representative of the major trends and points of articulation in the political and social life of Spain between 1939 and 1982. Of course, their relations with those various realities are too complex to be explained simply in the terms of social or historical determinism; in order to be appreciated in full, they require consideration also from alternative theoretical perspectives sited in literary and film criticism. From the available range of methods and approaches which promise to illuminate our subject, we propose to draw on the following: formalism (whose business is to identify significant patterns of, say, imagery or narrative organisation in particular works of art); structuralism and semiology (with their emphasis on the rule-bound and conventional nature of all processes of signification, and their view of literature as a system of intertextual relations); psychoanalysis (which, in one of its variant forms, brings to bear on the study of art a set of concepts deriving from Freudian theory, including the Oedipus complex, the death-wish and the Reality principle, as well as an interest in dreams and the conditions of instinctual repression, the eternal conflict between primary and secondary thought processes, between id and superego, in the formation of the self); and, finally, theories of ideology, as exemplified in the work of writers such as Louis Althusser. Althusser's conception of «ideology» as that set of attitudes which most people unconsciously adopt towards self and society in ordinary life, «the imaginary relationship of individuals to their real conditions of existence»,[12] provides a theoretical basis for our investigation of the impact of dictatorship ideology on cultural activity in Spain during the period which concerns us. By simultaneously pursuing these parallel lines of enquiry, we hope to be able to account for the most important aspects of the texts selected for examination here.

It may not be redundant to remark at this point that the images of contemporary Spain which are projected in novels like *La colmena* and *Tiempo*

---

[11] In a controversial and closely contested decision made public on 17 April 1985, the *Tribunal Constitucional* ruled that a Bill on abortion proposed by Felipe González's Socialist administration and already approved by the *Cortes* was unconstitutional.

[12] See LOUIS ALTHUSSER's «Ideology and the State», in *Lenin and Philosophy and Other Essays*, translated by Ben Brewster (London, 1977), p. 153.

de silencio and in films like Borau's *Furtivos* and Saura's *Stress* do not function as unmediated representations of socio-political phenomena, but rather are the products of complex and problematical cultural processes. *Tiempo de silencio,* for example, recreates a microcosm of mid-century Madrid in a richly varied language whose multiple connotations have consistently resisted dogmatic, simple-minded interpretation. From one point of view, therefore, the novel represents an outstanding achievement on the part of a highly individualistic author who succeeded in expressing a personal vision of Spain in an elaborate and elusive symbolic idiom. Yet, we must not underestimate the constraints, both political and cultural, within which Luis Martín Santos lived and worked, nor overlook the essential paradox of *Tiempo de silencio* which, even as it searches for an authentic voice, fragments into a plurality of registers and accents whose origins lie in sources as diverse as universal mythology, the native literary tradition (Cervantes, Ortega y Gasset), and numerous categories of discourse (e. g. legal discourse) regarded traditionally as inimical to the creative spirit but now revealed to be susceptible to the most inventive forms of parody. Needless to say, no single one of these assumed voices can be attributed unequivocally to the historical figure of Martín Santos. A similar observation must be made about *Si te dicen que caí* where Juan Marsé intertwines the voices of a large number of not always clearly differentiated characters from several locations in recent Spanish history, with the aim of articulating the consciousness of an anonymous collectivity silenced by the experience of hardship and repression spread over three decades of Francoism. Marsé's commentators agree that this is an accurate appraisal of how his novel works, but certain contradictions in statements made by Marsé on the very question of the book's political intent introduce a disconcerting element into the task of its explication.

What we are outlining here is a problematical view of the relation between the conventional notion of authorial hegemony and the restraints jointly imposed on novelists, dramatists, film directors, etc. by artistic convention and ideology. [13] One of the most vibrant developments in current understanding of film and literature is a growing awareness of the complexity and intractability of this issue which is perhaps illustrated most tellingly in the debate conducted in circles of film criticism between the exponents of «auteurism», who typically argue the centrality of the author/director's role in a film's production, and those for whom his position is severely circumscribed, both by ideological factors and by the working conditions of film art which is quintessentially a collaborative venture. [14] In the context of our present choices Buñuel and Saura are two examples of directors who perhaps

---

[13] JONATHAN CULLER considers the force of convention in art in *Structuralist Poetics* (London, 1975).

[14] See ANDREW SARRIS, «Notes on the *Auteur* Theory in 1962», *Film Culture*, No. 27 (Winter 1962-63), 1-8.

more than most in the history of the cinema have succeeded in leaving their mark very firmly on the films they have directed. Co-scripting their films, insisting on editorial rights, working with regular personnel, they have each managed to avoid the humiliations that directors as famous as Hitchcock, Lang, Welles and Wilder, working in different conditions of production, suffered in the cutting rooms. [15] Following the «auteurist» line, it is quite plain that the private attitudes and preoccupations of both Buñuel and Saura create well-defined patterns over the whole range of their careers; Buñuel, as everyone has pointed out, returns over and over again to the Surrealists' obsession with, for instance, dreams, sadism, religion and sexual repression; his inimitable wit and brisk cinematic style are features of all the films, even though the extreme degradations of his personal vision, so constant a motif in his early films, are by the time of his later ones balanced by a more tolerant attitude towards the bourgeois values that to a large degree inspired them. Saura, too, with his socio-political obsessions, his fondness for role-playing, collages, dynasties and so on is clearly a director whose presence is very marked in all the films he has made. And yet, while *Viridiana, Stress* and *Carmen* can indeed be understood in terms of their representation of their directors' known thematic and formal idiosyncrasies, they also articulate in ways that may ultimately lie beyond their directors' conscious aims the mood of an entire culture at crucial moments in its history. *Viridiana,* Buñuel's first film in Spain after the long years of exile, merges the enduring interests of the eternal surrealist with the complex reflections of a repressive society tempted by «apertura» yet still pinned down by death-dealing conventions. *Stress,* an unjustly neglected film by the inheritor of Buñuel's artistic legacy, is Saura's 60s evocation of a society harbouring destructive instincts which, it suggests, may not be contained indefinitely. And *Carmen* is the testimony of a nation attempting to pick up the pieces of its lost identity, striving to regain its place in the wider European community yet still inevitably anchored in the grim realities of the recent past.

A film, no less than any other work of art, is the product of historical circumstance and, as we are arguing here, in some senses, the child of ideology; sometimes it may consciously or unconsciously challenge established structures of values (as in Buñuel's *El discreto encanto de la burguesía*), at others it acquiesces in them (as in Ladislao Vajda's *Marcelino, pan y vino* [1955]). Sometimes the borderline between conformity and rejection is very hard to define: in *Stress,* for example, does the film take for granted that the wife should nurse her husband's wounds because she is a woman, or does it dramatise this ideological assumption in order to expose it? In *Viridiana,* does the film innocently assume that housemaids will not only be women but will also service their male masters sexually, or does it draw

---

[15] See, e. g., on *Suspicion,* DANIEL SPOTO, *The Art of Alfred Hitchcock, 50 Years of the Motion Pictures* (London, 1977), p. 116.

7

these assumptions to our attention precisely so that we can see for ourselves the workings of an insidious ideology? Where in more firmly «auteurist» times questions like these would have been answered in ways reflecting confidence in the director's control over a film's range of meanings, now the legacy of the post-structuralist, deconstructive climate makes the uniqueness of the singular vision an increasingly problematic concept.

Moreover, the collaborative foundations and processes characteristic of film art are a further complicating factor. One could argue, à propos of *Viridiana,* and quite apart from the contribution of the co-script writer (Julio Alejandro), the director of photography (José Aguayo), the art director (Francisco Canet), etc., that Buñuel's enforced use of Silvia Pinal in the title role is one very clear piece of evidence that the film is not entirely his own creative property. The choice of this actress, like those of the principals in *Abismos de pasión* and of Catherine Deneuve in *Tristana,* was on each occasion the producer's. [16] In an art form where the visual dimensions are so unarguably dominant, the director's intentions are in such circumstances immediately inflected by events outside his control. For in each case the actress brings not only her skills as a performer —which she will use to greater or lesser effect in her interpretation of the part— but also her embeded, coded meanings in a persona as much the product and projection of her culture as of her own inherited, native characteristics. Deneuve and Pinal perhaps rose to such heights of popularity by being, as Molly Haskell puts it in a discussion of Deneuve, «so bland and static» at a time, the 60s, when blandness and stasis were so greatly prized, above all as attributes associated with women. [17] In an age that revered the fashion model —the implications of which we take up and treat more fully in our chapter on *Stress*— it was not unexpected that icons of female beauty should look like High Street shop window dummies. Buñuel, then, has no alternative, once Pinal is assigned to the role of Viridiana by the executive producer, other than to accommodate his own preconceptions of her place in the film's narrative to the persona that will inevitably, and partially, mould the character. Even though he may well, as Molly Haskell again notes, draw out and comment on potentialities of persona with all the skill and sensitivity of an unfailingly brilliant creative intelligence, in the end there is always something that evades his control, something enabling the actress to speak, not only for herself as an individual, but also representatively, either consciously or unconsciously, as a mouthpiece for the age. [18]

The principles we are formulating here hold true for art forms other than film, so as we turn our thoughts to the novel we take notice of Roland

---

[16] See AGUSTÍN SÁNCHEZ VIDAL, *Luis Buñuel. Obra Cinematográfica* (Madrid, 1984), pp. 179-80; p. 327.

[17] See MOLLY HASKELL, *From Reverence to Rape. The Treatment of Women in the Movies* (New York, 1973).

[18] See MOLLY HASKELL, op. cit., p. 305.

Barthes' idea of «the death of the author». [19] In advancing his controversial claim, Barthes set out to subvert traditional assumptions concerning the primacy of an author's intentions, the coherence and uniqueness of his vision and the degree of control which any creative writer may be deemed to exercise over the subject matter and procedures employed in his work. Without feeling obliged to accept all of the most radical implications of Barthes' bold metaphor, we find, in the theoretical context described here, equal measures of coherence and relevance in an argument that sees the literary author as an agent or medium through which a community's collective preoccupations may be articulated. Isaac Montero observes pertinently, in a survey of developments in Spanish fiction in the early 60s, that «Tras toda búsqueda innovadora [en la novela] hay la necesidad de dar expresión a una temática y a una preocupación colectivas». [20] This does not, of course, mean that the literature of an age is a monolithic structure lacking in diversity, rather, that it gives expression to a communal voice splintered into a multitude of accents whose distinctiveness will be proportional to the individuality of the signature or imprint which each author leaves on his or her work.

In our study of novels by Martín Santos, Caballero Bonald and Marsé and films by Buñuel and Saura, we shall have an opportunity to test this model of criticism. The texts selected for examination here lend themselves particularly well to investigation from the points of view rehearsed above. On the one hand, all six works display intrinsic features of note: already recognised as landmarks in the development of contemporary Spanish film and fiction, *Tiempo de silencio*, *Viridiana*, *Si te dicen que caí* and *Carmen* have attracted a good deal of serious critical attention and still retain a vital capacity to awaken fresh interest; we believe *Dos días de setiembre* and *Stress* to be works of equally impressive formal and conceptual complexity that deserve a substantial re-evaluation. On the other hand, these literary and film texts share some fundamental similarities, foremost among which is an underlying visual orientation. Every one of the novels discussed here incorporates visual material into the verbal fabric of its construction. Two of the authors concerned are closely associated with the world of the cinema: José Manuel Caballero Bonald as the script-writer of *El balcón abierto* —directed by Jaime Camino in 1984— and Juan Marsé, both as a script-writer, in collaboration with Camino in the preparation of *1945* —a film made in the year of General Franco's death— and as the author of some perceptive vignettes of film personalities including Marlon Brando, John Wayne, Carlos Saura, Geraldine Chaplin, and Brigitte Bardot. [21] Marsé is also a dedicated film buff whose extensive knowledge of cinema is condensed in essay form —see his prologue to *Imágenes y recuerdos 1949-1960*.

---

[19] ROLAND BARTHES, *Image, Music, Text*. Essays selected and translated by Stephen Heath (London, 1977), pp. 142-48.
[20] ISAAC MONTERO, «La novela española de 1955 hasta hoy», p. 95.
[21] See JUAN MARSÉ, *Señoras y señores* (Barcelona, 1977).

Tiempo de satélites[22]— and constantly brought into play in his creative work. A second visual aspect of the novels is their inclusion of pictorial references. One such reference contained in *Si te dicen que caí* reappears in *Stress* by Carlos Saura, thus providing a coincidence which holds out the prospect of further discoveries of substantial interrelationships between the texts examined here.

We begin our analysis by looking at the novels one by one, and then proceed to a study of the films. This method will allow us not only to establish points of similarity, but also to trace some of the developments that have taken place within the spheres of film and fiction which, in our opinion, encompass the highest and most significant achievements of Spanish art in recent decades.

---

[22] See *Imágenes y recuerdos 1949-1960. Tiempo de satélites,* with a prologue by JUAN MARSÉ (Barcelona, 1976).

1

DOS DÍAS DE SETIEMBRE: THE NIGHTMARE OF HISTORY

The award of the Biblioteca Breve prize of 1961 to José Manuel Caballero Bonald for his novel, *Dos días de setiembre,* signalled the author's emergence as a leading figure in the «generación del medio siglo». [1] Two subsequent novels, *Ágata, ojo de gato* (Premio de la Crítica, 1975) and *Toda la noche oyeron pasar pájaros* (Premio Ateneo de Sevilla, 1984), as well as several volumes of poetry, have consolidated Caballero Bonald's reputation and sustained a remarkable record of critical and financial success. *Dos días de setiembre* in particular continues to sell well: a definitive edition of 1979 containing revisions of the 1962 original was reprinted in 1984, and boosted the total number of sales in Spain, France, Rumania and Czechoslovakia to over 70.000. [2] Widespread critical acknowledgement of the importance of Caballero Bonald's novel complements this statistical evidence of its continuing commercial appeal. For Ignacio Soldevila Durante, author of a comprehensive overview of Spanish fiction since 1936, *Dos días de setiembre* «es una de las mejores [novelas] de la época que nos toca analizar». [3] Several commentators note the book's importance in the evolution of Spanish fiction in the post-Civil War period. Juan Carlos Curutchet claims that it is «un jalón fundamental en [el] proceso evolutivo de la narrativa española»; [4] Elías Díaz brackets it together with three other titles (*Tiempo de silencio* by Luis Martín Santos, *Los enanos* by Concha Alós, and *Año tras año* by Armando López Salinas) which, in his opinion, exemplify «[una] situación de cambio, de polémica y crisis del realismo» in a period of transition in

---

[1] The label «generación del medio siglo» was first proposed by José María Castellet in «La novela española quince años después (1942-1957)», *Cuadernos del Congreso por la Libertad de la Cultura,* 33 (November-December 1958), 48-52.

[2] We are grateful to Sr. Caballero Bonald and to his agent, Doña Carmen Balcells, for supplying this factual information.

[3] IGNACIO SOLDEVILA DURANTE, *La novela desde 1936,* Historia de la literatura española actual, II (Madrid, 1980), p. 286.

[4] JUAN CARLOS CURUTCHET, *Cuatro ensayos sobre la nueva novela española* (Montevideo, 1973), p. 26.

Spain; [5] and José Ortega stresses the novel's innovations vis à vis the stylistic conventions of the time. [6]

Interpretation of *Dos días de setiembre* has developed along lines familiar to students of other Spanish novels of the 1950s and 60s, notably, *El Jarama,* by Rafael Sánchez Ferlosio, and *Gran Sol,* by Ignacio Aldecoa. [7] Reviewing *Dos días de setiembre* in the pages of *Ínsula,* Ricardo Doménech argued that «esta primera novela de Caballero Bonald se encuentra dentro de las líneas generales —inconformismo, denuncia social, etc.— que caracterizan la nueva novela y en general la nueva literatura española». Doménech's view of *Dos días de setiembre* as primarily a novel of characters who represent «los distintos estamentos sociales que configuran una colectividad rural española» [8] typifies the prejudices and priorities of contemporary literary debate. For, as numerous authors, including Caballero Bonald, proclaimed their allegiance to the tenets of social realism and made known their ambition to write «la novela que las circunstancias exigen: la vinculada a la realidad nacional y la que se propone como norma específica reproducir unos hechos de muy concreto matiz español», [9] so a majority of commentators responded by interpreting their work both in terms of a commitment to the cause of social reform and with regard to the verisimilitude of their depictions of life in the towns and countryside of Spain. [10] Inconsistencies in declarations of principle, retractions from previously stated positions (as in the case of Caballero Bonald), [11] and noticeable discomfort with prescribed guidelines

---

[5] ELÍAS DÍAZ, *Pensamiento español 1939-1975,* second edition (Madrid, 1978), p. 238.

[6] JOSÉ ORTEGA, «Estilo y nueva narrativa española», in *Actas del Sexto Congreso Internacional de Hispanistas* (Toronto, Canada, 1980), 547-51.

[7] We refer to the discrepant views of, on the one hand, those critics who emphasise the socio-historical, documentary features of works of fiction and, on the other, those who discern the presence of poetic and symbolic elements in the text. Francisco García Sarriá reconciles opposing readings of SÁNCHEZ FERLOSIO's famous novel in «El Jarama. Muerte y merienda de Lucita», *BHS,* LIII (1976), 323-37. JACK B. JELINSKI challenges exclusively mimetic readings of *Gran Sol* in «A Critical Re-examination of *Gran Sol*», in *Ignacio Aldecoa: a Collection of Critical Essays,* ed. RICARDO LANDEIRA and CARLOS MELLIZO (Laramie, Wyoming, 1977), pp. 41-47.

[8] RICARDO DOMÉNECH, «*Dos días de setiembre* y la nueva novela», *Ínsula,* 193 (December 1962), p. 4.

[9] See CABALLERO BONALD's declarations to José Luis Cano reproduced in *Ínsula,* 185 (April 1962), p. 5.

[10] See the arguments of JOAQUÍN MARCO in his essay, «En torno a la novela social española», *Ínsula,* 202 (September 1963), p. 13.

[11] There is a revealing contrast between declarations which CABALLERO BONALD made in 1962 and others from the period 1969-70. He informed the authors of a survey and questionnaire published under the title «Panorama du roman espagnol» in *Les Lettres Françaises,* July 1962, that, in composing *Dos días de setiembre,* he had sought to «reflect» the reality of Spain «avec la plus grande objectivité possible» because «cette reproduction objective de la réalité est la seule formule valable pour permettre a l'écrivain de remplir son rôle social» (p. 4). However, in an interview conducted by FEDERICO CAMPBELL and published in *Infame turba* (Barcelona, 1971), he remarked that «Nunca tuve la intención de fabricar ninguna clase de reportaje» and insisted that «la validez esencial de la literatura, con independencia de todas sus demás categorías morales, sociales, etcétera, radica en su validez como obra de arte, que es la única

indicate that the orthodoxy of social realism was more apparent than real. [12] Novels like *Tormenta de verano,* by Juan García Hortelano, and *La zanja,* by Alfonso Grosso, provide reassuring evidence of the disparity between theoretical statements of intent and the practical achievements of authors at work, and illustrate the capacity which literary imagination and language have to break out of a straitjacket of crude ideology. [13] But, if an oversimplified view of literature and social reality failed to stifle all creative instincts in Spain in the 1950s and early 60s, it nevertheless had a serious inhibiting effect on critical thinking, spawning a second-order «crude reflective realism» [14] which continued to enjoy currency long after the social realist mode of writing had gone out of fashion.

Over a period of almost twenty years *Dos días de setiembre* has been the object of reductive literal-minded readings. In an extensive essay published in 1968, Pablo Gil Casado remarked on «el logrado realismo, la técnica lenta, la visión total y la casi perfecta integración de lo documental y del elemento ficcional» in the book, and expressed admiration for Caballero Bonald's powers of observation and realistic character portrayal. The main part of Gil Casado's study consists of an analysis of the characters of *Dos días de setiembre*. These he divides into four groups: «los ricos cosecheros [de la vendimia], sus intermediarios, los hijos de los primeros, y los jornaleros», which he sees as being interconnected by «una serie ... de conflictos de signo moral y social, que se muestran testimonialmente para poner en evidencia las injusticias sociales y la correspondiente crítica [por parte del autor]». [15] Caballero Bonald confirms that, in writing *Dos días de setiembre,* he had sought to «acusar para moralizar, limitándome a presentar unos hechos y unas circunstancias de los que he sido riguroso testigo». [16] Gil Casado also correctly highlights the roles of Joaquín, alias el Guita, the unfortunate gypsy with whose death the narrative reaches a tragic climax, and Miguel Gamero, an alcoholic clerk in a wine export business who is characterised by a profound spiritual malaise. However, on balance his essay displays an excessive degree of concern with the «authenticity» of the social types and the Andalusian setting of *Dos días de setiembre*. The result is a

---

que llega a sortear las amenazas de deterioro del tiempo o de las modas», (pp. 316 & 319).

[12] See the critical observations made by SANTOS SANZ VILLANUEVA in *Historia de la novela social española (1942-75)*, 2 vols. (Madrid, 1980), I, 112-223, and FERNANDO MORÁN's assessment in *Explicación de una limitación: La novela realista de los años 50 en España* (Madrid, 1971).

[13] FRANCISCO GARCÍA SARRIÁ has evaluated García Hortelano's artistic achievement (pace JUAN CARLOS CURUTCHET) in «*Tormenta de verano*: Abandono y despojo de Maruja, alias Margot», *Neophilologus*, LXVI (1982), 227-34.

[14] This phrase is used by JOHN BUTT in his trenchant study, *Writers and Politics in Modern Spain* (London, 1978), p. 54.

[15] PABLO GIL CASADO, *La novela social española (1920-1971)*, second edition (Barcelona, 1973), pp. 267 & 273.

[16] See CABALLERO BONALD's declarations to JOSÉ LUIS CANO reproduced in *Insula*, 185 (April 1962), p. 5.

certain superficiality of response which has serious consequences for a proper understanding of the novel. Santos Sanz Villanueva's study of 1980 bears this stricture out. Sanz Villanueva signals the admirable intention to account as much for «el innegable talento narrativo y la densidad lingüística de Caballero Bonald» as for the thematic richness of his novel, but a methodological-conservatism generally confines him to making observations about «el carácter modélico de los sucesos», «el carácter paradigmático [de los personajes]» and the virtues of «un diálogo veraz» in the book. [17] The date of publication of Sanz Villanueva's study testifies to the surprising longevity of a critical approach which appears doomed to repeat predictable conclusions.

The persistence of such readings is all the more remarkable when one considers that a counter-trend was established as early as 1971 with the publication of Juan Carlos Curutchet's pioneering essay, «Caballero Bonald: un precursor». This critic discovers not mimetic, but poetic values in *Dos días de setiembre* which he forthrightly claims «es una de las novelas que implican la abolición de una persistente y anacrónica falacia estética y el descubrimiento de la *terra ignota* de unas posibilidades verbales inéditas, inexploradas hasta entonces». For Curutchet, the strengths of the novel lie predominantly beneath its surface and include an allusive treatment of social and political themes, a rich verbal texture and a poetic framework in which two elements —«El Vino» and «El Levante» (the east wind)— «cob[ran] un nítido cariz simbólico», the first connoting a dark world of suffering, the second symbolising «la Conciencia o la evidencia de la Condena». Here *Dos días de setiembre* is no longer seen as a photographic representation of conditions in an Andalusian town but rather as an investigation «de tipo histórico-psicológico» into the latent realities of Franco's Spain. [18] Curutchet's stimulating *aperçus* were largely ignored until Ignacio Soldevila Durante re-examined *Dos días de setiembre* and concluded that «el aspecto fundamental» of the book is its «visión esencialmente poética [de] una sociedad estática en la que la podredumbre y la fermentación de los más bajos instintos antisociales envenenan todo, desde la atmósfera hasta las entrañas mismas de la tierra». Soldevila Durante's interpretation established once and for all that, in its depiction of a social and natural background against which the characters' experience unfolds, *Dos días de setiembre* is not a sociological document but a highly wrought «novela poemática». [19]

Breaking the mould of literal-minded readings, Soldevila Durante's study emphasises the processes of mediation whereby a work of fiction becomes a symbolic projection of historical reality. Some of his remarks, particularly à propos of imagery of disease, may serve as a useful starting point for an

---

[17] SANZ VILLANUEVA, *Historia de la novela social española (1942-75)*, II, 689-98.
[18] CURUTCHET, *Cuatro ensayos sobre la nueva novela española*, pp. 25, 21 & 11.
[19] SOLDEVILA DURANTE, *La novela desde 1936*, pp. 284-86.

analysis of aspects of *Dos días de setiembre* which illustrate Caballero Bonald's achievements in this regard. We propose to consider the symbolism of disease in connexion with psychological, social and historical factors, then to inquire into the significance of the death of Joaquín and his relation to other characters, and, finally, to examine hitherto neglected elements in the figurative design of the text. Such an analysis may illuminate the extraordinary complexity of this novel while helping to clarify its position in Caballero Bonald's overall output and elucidating its relation to other works of the period.

An analysis of the various illnesses from which characters suffer in *Dos días de setiembre* reveals a widespread pattern of personal and collective sickness. Irrespective of their standing in the author's eyes, individuals are made to suffer the effects of diabetes (Ayuso), arthritis (Serafín), hypertension (Don Gabriel), vertigo (Don Andrés), asthma (Ayuso), and other bronchial conditions (Serafín, Don Gabriel, Lucas). Diseases of the skin, visible in the marks and scars which many of the characters display, constitute a fourth category after those affecting the head, chest and stomach. Miguel Gamero exemplifies an all-pervasive organic sickness. «Hace un par de años», he boasts, «podía romper con una simple inspiración una cadena atada al pecho», [20] but now, at the age of forty, he has to contend with «un agrio empellón de bilis [que] se me agolpa en el pecho, trepando dolorosamente hacia la nuca a medida que cae la noche» (124). He complains of «las larvas del alcohol [que] me están royendo el vientre» (113) and makes light of the risk of hepatitis (112). An even greater concentration of maladies is found in the figure of Joaquín, «el hombre del lobanillo», who is introduced in the first paragraph of the novel: «Tenía las orejas gachas y un protuberante lobanillo en la sien, que se le disparaba como una tumefacta erupción por entre los lacios mechones del pelo» (13). The «amoratada excrecencia» (42) which disfigures his forehead resembles the stigmata of other characters including Marcelo, Ayuso's son, who «era pecoso y rubiasco, con una gran mancha colorada asomándole por el cuello» (75). Joaquín is prone to attacks of vertigo (205) and experiences continual abdominal discomfort associated with an ulcer (101-02). Chest pains (17) complete the repertoire of his symptomatic disorders and anticipate his death underneath a «bota llena de mosto [que] pesa más de quinientos kilos» (288): «Joaquín ni siquiera dejó escapar un quejido; tampoco se hubiese notado a través de la madera. Sólo se oyó el derrumbe de los huesos y una como silbante salida de líquido por los boquetes de las costillas» (281).

In this characterisation of a sick community Caballero Bonald reserves particularly strong physical images, those of vomit and excrement, for his

---

[20] JOSÉ MANUEL CABALLERO BONALD, *Dos días de setiembre* (Barcelona: Editorial Argos Vergara, 1979), p. 57. Hereafter page references to this edition of the novel are cited in the text.

portrayal of Miguel and Joaquín. Joaquín vomits copiously on the first night of the action and again on the second when «se volcó sobre el pilón [del pozo], vomitando a violentas y convulsas tarascadas»; moments later, «se metió sin darse cuenta en el estiércol» and mutters recriminatingly to himself «Soy un mierda» (207). Miguel had previously proclaimed, on a group visit to the Valdecañizo estate,

> Soy el último eslabón de una cadena de ilustres traficantes de letrinas... Soy el que soy... Miradme bien antes de que represente la historia de los míos... Con un fusil de palo... Toda mi maldita casta con un fusil de palo... Cambiaron mierda por mierda... Todas las cañerías están atascadas de mierda... (60)

He, like Joaquín, finds relief from routine hangovers through vomiting: «No hay otro remedio que vomitar, eso alivia», he thinks (229).

Together, these two characters represent extreme forms of sickness. They also carry within themselves diseases which are hereditary: their *damnosa hereditas* and that of society as a whole are preserved within a caste structure (the word «casta» appears on pp. 60, 85, 104 & 107), and manifest themselves in clearly defined physical and spiritual terms. The dominant symptom of the community's distemper is an aggressive and perverse sexual lust illustrated in the history of the Varela family. Rafael imagines his father, Don Gabriel, «persiguiendo a las criadas de su casa, con los ojos supurados de vino, la boca rijosa y despreciativa». He has visions, too, of «su propia y hereditaria lujuria rebuscando desconcertadamente por el cuerpo de Matilde. El implacable contagio que había tenido que ir extirpándose como un pus desde que era casi un niño» (164-65). The memory of sexual relations with Matilde, who «no pierde el tiempo, lo mismito que su madre» (97-98), is as disturbing to Rafael as Miguel's continuing remorse over his lecherous uncle Felipe's abuse of Encarnita is to him.

Rancour (200), submissiveness (95), apathy (160) and a diffuse sense of guilt (113) are the spiritual counterparts of the community's physical malaise and a copy-book example of the «discontents of civilization». Sigmund Freud's vision of human life in terms of instinctual conflict, anxiety and aggression acquires graphic expression in Caballero Bonald's novel. Miguel's dream after his seduction by Encarnita, at the age of fourteen, reveals a traumatic sense of guilt accompanied by fears of punishment and an identification of the erotic with death:

> Y crecía la parte de abajo de la cómoda, arrastrándose a todo lo largo del tabique y trepando por las paredes hasta la cuña de una viga chorreante de pelos y de alquitrán, y crecía la banca de la capilla del colegio, anillándose como una boa sobre el órgano, derramándose por el comulgatorio, tapando los dos altares del muro lateral, y crecía mi cuerpo como el sexo de un garañón, enroscándose en el cuerpo de Encarnita, que tenía la cara de la prima Lupe, y la prima Lupe abría la boca delante de mis ojos, con la lengua fuera como una ahorcada. (141)

Joaquín's violent outburst in *el tabanco de Manuel* where he draws a knife and threatens the bar-tender (42-46) bears the hallmark of irrationality. It takes his companion, Lucas, completely by surprise and ends as unexpectedly as it had begun: «El hombre del lobanillo cambió el tono inesperadamente, como si se estuviera aburriendo de todo aquello y despertara de pronto a la realidad» (45).

The source of the collective neurosis described here is located to a large extent in social, cultural and economic structures, following Herbert Marcuse's assertion that «The reality principle materializes in a system of institutions». [21] In the case of Miguel, it is the *padre director* at his boarding school who acts as an agent of repression, with consequences identical to those outlined by Freud. «When an instinctual trend undergoes repression», Freud observes, «its libidinal elements are turned into symptoms, and its aggressive components into a sense of guilt». [22] Upon reaching the age of twenty, Miguel resumes sexual relations with Encarna who, from that moment on,

> fue para mí como una especie de vengativa escapada hacia no sabía dónde, como algo sucio pero verdadero a pesar de su aparente suciedad. Me daba la impresión de que así vivía todo lo que me habían negado antes. (230)

Joaquín's social and cultural circumstances are likewise major determinants of his neurotic disposition. Like Sebastián Vázquez in *Con el viento solano* by Ignacio Aldecoa, [23] Joaquín is a gypsy whose marginal status is compounded by the fact that he is not even a native of mainland Spain, but a *forastero* who comes «del mismo Moro» in Spanish north Africa (42). His nickname, «El Guita» (a colloquial term meaning «cash»), sums up his role as a serviceable object in a community which provides only sporadic opportunities for employment. A history of social segregation and economic exploitation accounts substantially for his reaction of cowardice and impotence when Don Gabriel abuses him at a party in La Damajuana bar:

> Joaquín se fue detrás de don Gabriel tragándose la quina, conteniéndose como quizá nunca se había contenido. Cuando se aguantaba se ponía enfermo de rencor, se le enconaba en el pecho su temple humillado... Ahora hubiera dado cualquier cosa por tener una última reserva de arrestos, como la noche anterior en el tabanco de Manuel, cuando buscaba la bronca incluso de una forma gratuita, para vengarse de la propia imposición de su cobardía. (200)

---

[21] HERBERT MARCUSE, *Eros and Civilization* (London, 1973), p. 31.

[22] SIGMUND FREUD, «Civilization and its Discontents», in *Civilization, Society and Religion, Group Psychology, Civilization and its Discontents and Other Works*. The Pelican Freud Library, vol. 12. Trans. from the German under the general editorship of James Strachey (Harmondsworth, 1985), p. 332.

[23] For an analysis of *Con el viento solano*, see ROBIN FIDDIAN, *Ignacio Aldecoa*, Twayne's World Authors Series, 529 (Boston, 1979), pp. 54-63.

Joaquín clearly resents Don Gabriel's overbearing authority but submits to it in a spirit of «agobiante y angustioso rencor» (231) indicative of a masochistic tendency born of repeated social victimization.

The weight of the past rests heavily on the characters of *Dos días de setiembre*. Miguel's need to «vomitar de una vez el asqueroso cieno de [la] memoria» (125) underlines the significance of past experience as a burden which must be discharged in order to attain physical and spiritual health. In a typical moment of depression Miguel relives details of his youth, including his uncle Felipe's misuse of the proceeds of the sale of the family home and his relations with his cousin Lupe, as «la memoria de la estafa y del fracaso. Las iracundas espiras de vacío de sus cuarenta años de vida. Todo eso junto y nada. Nada» (275). The world of collective historical experience further condenses «la áspera tiniebla de [la] memoria» (113), with the Spanish Civil War and its aftermath looming as prominent points of reference in the lives of the inhabitants. The post-war years are evoked through a variety of characters and narrative techniques. A third person narrator sketches compact biographical profiles of Don Andrés, Ayuso, Onofre, and Julián and Mateo Cobeña. He mentions Julián's struggle to «librarse del hambre sirviendo de intermediario en saneados asuntos de estraperlo» (84) and remarks that «Lo único que a Mateo no le habían enseñado a aguantar era el agobiante recuerdo de los días del rebusco, cuando recorría de punta a punta las viñas calcinadas, con el hambre mordiéndole las tripas» (85). Joaquín's experience is recounted at length in chapter eight of part two. Having fought on the Republican side in the battle for control of Málaga in the spring of 1937,[24] Joaquín was imprisoned in the Penal del Puerto de Santa María for a period of «tres años menos cuarenta días». On his release, «el alcalde del pueblo no había querido darle ... el salvoconducto de la cárcel» (102) without which he would not be able to secure a permanent job, and went so far as to refuse him permission to remain in the town. This arbitrary decision to effectively place Joaquín outside the law was conveyed to him in the mayor's office under the fixed and indifferent gaze of two figures of authority whom we assume to be General Franco and José Antonio Primo de Rivera: «Desde el muro de la izquierda, las figuras de dos cuadros miraban para Joaquín» (103). After his expulsion «Joaquín anduvo dando bandazos por donde Dios le dio a entender ... hasta que cayó por el pueblo y decidió no seguir adelante» (104).

Caballero Bonald discreetly records the historical moment which inaugurated the present régimen of political authority, land ownership and economic ascendancy in the area. The stone gateway to Don Gabriel's estate is decorated with two porcelain plaques, one of which displays the name «MON-

---

[24] The nationalists' capture of Málaga coincided with an offensive against Republican troops in the valley of El Jarama. See HUGH THOMAS, *The Spanish Civil War* (Harmondsworth, 1977), pp. 582-88.

TERRODILLA», while the other bears the inscription «AÑO MCMXXXIX» (144). Historical data are incorporated into the narrative with greater immediacy through monologues which reveal the deep impression of collective experience on personal consciousness. Miguel's ruminations in chapter ten of part one and chapter five of part two represent the fluid expulsion of memory. The first stream of recollections begins to flow as he falls asleep; the second, responding to «la urgente y deleitosa necesidad de ponerse a pensar a oscuras», gets underway to the fitting accompaniment of «un estruendo de agua por una cañería» (218). Images of sickness reappear in Miguel's evocation of the post-war period in the province of Cadiz: «La epidemia de tifus no llevaba camino de arreglarse. El piojo verde había hecho su agosto y por todas partes se veían gentes con el cuerpo acribillado por el exantema» (219). He remembers the prevalence of hunger, poverty and unemployment, and registers the general mood of post-war Spanish society:

> El recuerdo de la guerra todavía seguía sin sedimentar del todo. De cuando en cuando, bajaba desde la sierra como una avalancha de rencor. Una mañana apareció un hombre muerto en una esquina, con una cartilla de racionamiento enrollada y metida por la boca. (222)

A final detail of Miguel's monologue concerns his involvement in the Civil War alongside his fellow Nationalist, Perico Montaña: «En el invierno de 1937», he recalls,

> nos habíamos ido los dos al frente de Málaga. Perico ya había cumplido los dieciocho años, a mí me faltaba poco. La guerra nos cogió cuando terminamos el bachillerato y, entre una cosa y otra, no pudimos estudiar Derecho, que era lo que teníamos pensado... Al volver del frente, cada uno se dedicó a lo suyo. (220-21)

It is no coincidence that the following chapter of part two features Joaquín's drunken and disjointed memories about his participation in the war. Some commentators acknowledge that the stories of Miguel and Joaquín alternate and complement each other; [25] on close inspection it becomes apparent that their relationship is in fact one of near equivalence and duplication. Chapter six of part two establishes several points of similarity between the lives of the two men, starting with the fact that they are of virtually the same age. Joaquín reflects, «Tengo treinta y nueve años y estoy hecho un guiñapo» (232), while Miguel's observation that he was born in June 1920 means that, in the month of September 1960 in which the action

---

[25] IGNACIO SOLDEVILA DURANTE states that «El relato reposa sobre un doble eje de personajes: Joaquín y Miguel», *La novela desde 1936,* p. 285, and GONZALO SOBEJANO notes the presence, in *Dos días de setiembre,* of «anticipaciones, retrospecciones, simultaneidades, concordancias buscadas...», in an allusive study in *Novela española de nuestro tiempo (en busca del pueblo perdido),* second edition (Madrid, 1970), pp. 324-29 (329).

of the book is set, he is but some few months older than Joaquín. El Guita considers how «A los diecisiete años me fui al frente y tenía miedo como ahora» (232). Like Miguel and his present companion-in-hardship, Lucas, he had fought on the battlefields of Andalusia, but on the Republican side. After his death Lucas recalls how «En el frente de Málaga lo íbamos a matar sin saber que era él» (283), and Miguel is momentarily troubled by the same strange coincidence: «Le pasó por la cabeza un fugaz vislumbre del frente de Málaga, cuando se encontró allí con Lucas. Joaquín estaba del otro lado» (313). What Miguel does not realise is that Joaquín is an alter ego, an Abel to his Cain in the internecine conflict of Spain in the 30s and 40s.

The impact of history on the individual consciousness is illustrated most vividly in the form of dreams and nightmares. For these characters, as for others found throughout contemporary Spanish film and fiction (e. g. Luis in *La prima Angélica* by Carlos Saura, Ana in *El espíritu de la colmena* by Víctor Erice, and la Ramona in *Si te dicen que caí* by Juan Marsé), «History is a nightmare» from which bewildered individuals are trying to awake.[26] In this respect, the key element, hitherto inexplicably neglected by critics,[27] is Joaquín's recurrent bad dream in which he suffers the same horrible fate as befell a cousin of his in the Civil War. The nightmare is first mentioned in chapter four of part one when Joaquín tells Lucas that «Anoche soñé que me habían colgado de un árbol por los pies ...» and explains that «En la guerra, colgaron a un primo mío por los pies y lo reventaron a verga-jazos» (47). In conversation with his common-law wife, Lola, a few hours later, he adds that in his nightmare «me daban con una vara en la barriga». Her nonchalant reply in the form of a rhetorical question: «¿Otra vez el disco de tu primo?» (100) underlines the frequency with which the nightmare visits him. Thereafter, the image of «un hombre con las tripas fuera colgando de un árbol» (206) becomes a leitmotif in the narrative and a crucial element in the conceptual structure of the novel.

At a personal and rather superficial level, Joaquín's nightmare expresses his abiding horror at the obscene violence inflicted on a close relative in

---

[26] Stephen Dedalus remarks that «History is a nightmare from which I am tryng to awake», in *Ulysses* by JAMES JOYCE (Harmondsworth, 1969), p. 40. CABALLERO BO-NALD attests to the traumatic effects of scenes of violence from the Civil War on his own psychological development: «Cuando empezó la guerra», he told Rafael Borrás Betriu, «yo tenía nueve años, es decir, que también tenía una capacidad poco menos que religiosa para las más turbadoras fijaciones emocionales... Entreveo aún el atroz e imborrable trauma provocado por la secreta expedición infantil al sitio donde fusi-laban a quienes, desde mis nieblas educativas, consideraba enemigos.» Equally pertinent is his indication that «He contado alguna de esas experiencias en una novela mía y en varios poemas» (see RAFAEL BORRÁS BETRIU, *Los que no hicimos la guerra*, Barce-lona, 1971, p. 153), since the date of his declarations identifies that novel as *Dos días de setiembre*.

[27] PABLO GIL CASADO mentions Joaquín's bad dream but does not accommodate it in an overall interpretation of the book. See *La novela social española (1920-1971)*, pp. 280-81.

the Spanish Civil War. Its full psychological significance finally becomes apparent only at the moment of his death, an event which is remarkable not the least because Joaquín does nothing to avoid the barrel as it tumbles down on top of him, in a scene reminiscent of Simón Orozco's death in *Gran Sol* by Ignacio Aldecoa. [28] Joaquín's failure to take evasive action similar to that of Lucas who «estaba a su lado y se quitó a tiempo» suggests chilling complicity in a fate which, to his mind, is preordained. An examination of the manner of his death points up an eerie resemblance to that of his cousin: «el cuerpo de Joaquín aplastándose con el tonel encima» and oozing fluids «por los boquetes de las costillas» (281) inevitably brings to mind the image of his cousin's «barriga reventada a palos» (238). Two cruelly ironic remarks confirm a connexion between the men. On the first night of the action Joaquín protests angrily that «No aguanto que me tomen de primo» (43), unaware of the resounding ambiguity of his idiomatic words. And, a fellow gypsy who had neglected to help him at *la Damajuana* shouts a warning: «Eh, tú, primo, que se te va a cortar la digestión», as Joaquín sits by the roadside «agachando la cabeza como si algo estuviese a punto de caérsele encima» (239). Caballero Bonald's aesthetic effects are impressive and well-contrived here, but an observation on literary technique must not overshadow the crucial significance of Joaquín's death, namely, that it is a compulsive re-enactment of his cousin's fate, orchestrated at the level of the unconscious. Unable to tolerate a hostile society's impositions any longer, el Guita allows himself to be figuratively beaten into submission, thereby exemplifying «that compulsion to repeat which in many cases produces fixations to traumatic experiences in the past and a daemonic compulsion to bring suffering on oneself». [29] As the barrel begins to topple onto him, Joaquín yields to the pressures of the Freudian death instinct and re-directs inwards that force of aggression to which he had given outward expression on the previous day in *el tabanco de Manuel*. His death is effectively a suicide [30] like that of the *arrumbador* who, in Miguel's reminiscence of the post-war years, «entró en una taberna, se bebió una botella sin pestañear y sacó un cuchillo. Dijo que quien le llevase la contraria iba a tener que entendérselas con él. Nadie le llevó la contraria y entonces el arrumbador se metió el cuchillo por la barriga y se mató» (222). In both instances the only resolution to cumulative despair is shown to lie in self-destruction.

Joaquín's nightmare possesses political as well as personal significance, because it formulates an entire community's anxieties about the continuing

[28] ROBIN FIDDIAN discusses the implications of Simón Orozco's death in «Sobre los múltiples significados de *Gran Sol*, novela española del mar», *Cuadernos hispanoamericanos*, 367-68 (January-February 1981), 287-99.

[29] NORMAN O. BROWN, *Life against Death. The Psychoanalytical Meaning of History* (London, 1960), pp. 87-88.

[30] JUAN CARLOS CURUTCHET deliberates, in a footnote, as to whether Joaquín's death is a suicide or an accident, in *Cuatro ensayos sobre la nueva novela española*, p. 17.

effects of war and violence; in this way it facilitates the return of the repressed unconscious which Marcuse defines as «the tabooed and subterranean history of civilisation». [31] That history is identified, in *Dos días de setiembre*, with Joaquín and his cousin who, in their dual capacities as gypsies and former defenders of the Republican cause, epitomise the Other which was confined to the «áspera tiniebla» of political oblivion at the end of hostilities. This does not mean that the Other ceased to exist. According to psychoanalytic theory, repression cannot annihilate its object, rather, that which is banished to the realm of the unconscious exerts «ceaseless upward pressure» [32] until it eventually breaks through the orderly surface of civilised existence, producing an overpowering sense of dissatisfaction and guilt. In *Dos días de setiembre* these symptoms are associated with Rafael, Perico and Miguel, repentant victors of the Civil War. Miguel remembers how, after 1939, «Nunca me sentía tranquilo, esa era la verdad, como si hubiese hecho algo de lo que no podía liberarme hasta que no lo pagara de alguna forma» (220). His restlessness continues into the narrative present when he «sentía la culpa como una masa amorfa y descompuesta» (113). Joaquín's death makes a dramatic impression on all three men, but it is left to Onofre's son to admit that ultimate responsibility for the tragedy rests not with fate but with the entire community: «Le tocó a él», he states, «la culpa es de todos» (315). This character, who «había sido para Miguel una especie de inveterada representación de la hombría» (312) and a personification of «la buena fe y la entereza» (157), is at once the moral and political conscience of the group and the sole example of spiritual health in a uniformly diseased community. [33]

When Rafael Borrás Betriu interviewed the author in the late 60s, Caballero Bonald expressed the conviction that «La guerra civil es un hecho —o mejor, un organismo— todavía vivo [en] los resortes motrices de ese cuerpo histórico [que es] la postguerra». [34] His novel portrays the persistent and pernicious effects of recent history on both the body and the mind of Spain. The two, of course, are inseparable: Julián Cobeña points out to Joaquín that «la salud depende mayormente de aquí» at the same time as «se apuntaba la sién con un dedo» (105). The encysted tumour, or *lobanillo*, located on Joaquín's forehead stands out —literally— as a sign of his inner trauma, while the diseased body of the community bears equally conspicuous testimony to the impact of war on the collective psyche.

Latent violence, trauma and morbid sickness spill out onto the natural setting of Caballero Bonald's Andalusian town. Juan Carlos Curutchet and

---

[31] MARCUSE, *Eros and Civilization*, p. 31.
[32] NORMAN O. BROWN, *Life against Death*, p. 271.
[33] In conversation with JOSÉ LUIS CANO, CABALLERO BONALD insisted that «una difusa pero manifiesta esperanza», pervades *Dos días de setiembre*. See *Ínsula*, 185 (April 1962), p. 5.
[34] BORRÁS BETRIU, *Los que no hicimos la guerra*, p. 153.

Ignacio Soldevila Durante have noted that the vineyards and surrounding countryside which «parecía estar sin resuello» under a nauseating heat (70) constitute a figurative landscape. To be precise, the setting of *Dos días de setiembre* is part metonymic, part metaphoric. It functions metonymically inasmuch as it reproduces the physical symptoms of individual and collective sickness discussed above. In the author's Expressionist vision respiratory and abdominal disorders are superimposed on the outside world, as in the description of a narrow street along which Vicente and Rafael walk on the first night of the action: «[Vicente] abrió la boca como buscando el aire que se estancaba entre las sombrías paredes del callejón ... Soplaba por la otra boca del callejón una racha de aire pestilente» (22-23). On the second night, as he leaves *la Damajuana,* Joaquín listens to «el hondo y aborrascado *estertor* de la noche» (207) (our emphasis). The gradual development and eruption of a storm mirrors Joaquín's growing frustration and simulates the stages of a process of alcoholic poisoning which may culminate in the bursting of a vital organ. As abdominal sickness is projected onto the landscape, surrounding fields acquire the odour of «fruta podrida y ... ovario vegetal», and «el fétido paridero de la tierra» releases «un enervante turbión de malsanos y turbulentos gérmenes». The image of «la tierra [que] olía como si le hubieran abierto el vientre» (197) recreates Encarnita's rape by Felipe Gamero (she remembers how «sentí como si me hubieran abierto en canal», p. 137), and recalls the violent deaths of Joaquín's cousin and the *arrumbador* who committed suicide. Images of abortion and death heighten the sense of a nightmarish world that has found its fulfilment in reality: «se palpaba el sofoco de la noche; el húmedo y malsano cuajo de la luna chorreando como una placenta» (59); the wind blows in «morbid» gusts (90), and fermenting wine exudes a «morboso exhalo» which Julián Cobeña compares to the foul-smelling belches coming from Joaquín's stomach (198). Joaquín in fact smells fermenting must even though «no hay una viña en toda la redonda» (199), a curious detail which confirms that the landscape is an extension, or projection, of the characters' bodily sicknesses. A final instance of this practice is the description of *el pago de Monterrodilla* whose outstanding feature is a «protuberancia central» (143) which duplicates the «protuberante lobanillo» on Joaquín's forehead (13).

The setting of *Dos días de setiembre* functions metaphorically as a theatre (cf. «escenario», p. 21) in which the destructive violence of the Civil War is played out anew. The very first page of the book describes a vineyard dominated by a watch tower («bienteveo») which is subsequently shown to be an exact replica of Joaquín's war-time post; el Guita remembers spending «toda la noche en el bienteveo, acechando para que nadie se acerque. Dos años largos tiritando de miedo en las trincheras» (231). In the same opening chapter, when he and Lucas are shot at by the guard on duty and hear «el último disparo ... absorbiendo los huidizos ecos del primero, tableteando cada vez más débilmente en la distancia» (18), he associates «el angustioso

23

fogonazo del disparo, el líquido escozor de la sal encaramándose por el muslo, la desolada y amenazante negrura de la viña, la trinchera» (48). Gunfire, «un tableteo de matraca» (192) and the peals of thunder which ring out like «lejanos fusilazos» when the storm finally breaks (207) recreate the sounds of war with unmistakeable clarity in the narrative present. This superimposition of events from different historical contexts is a common feature of the mental processes of several characters, including Miguel who «confundía los hechos de hacía algunas horas con otros más lejanos y martirizantes»; Caballero Bonald exploits the same procedure of «imágenes superpuestas» (113) in his elaboration of this intricately constructed book.

The author enhances the symbolic design of his novel by inscribing it within a Christian paradigm. Like Paco, el del molino in *Réquiem por un campesino español* (1953) by Ramón Sender, Joaquín is portrayed as a Christ-figure: he dies on a Friday afternoon at 15:00 hours (288); the pointedly named Serafín twice exclaims «Cristo» as he approaches the corpse moments after the accident (282). Although the «día de autos, el de la fecha» falls in September and not in Holy Week (283), it nevertheless coincides with the Exaltation of the Holy Cross on 14 September. Joaquín's death thus fits the mould of Christ's Passion and acquires an aura of archetypal martyrdom. The description of a *bodega* «dividida en cuatro naves, igual que la planta de una iglesia» (177), and a profusion of sacramental imagery of blood and wine (41, 281) reinforce the paradigm and in retrospect illuminate Joaquín's gesture of licking the palm of his hand «hasta que le supo a vinagre» (16).

The motif of the well, which is prominent in Christian lore, is also incorporated into the narrative of *Dos días de setiembre* but in an unorthodox way, its conventional connotations of baptism, purification and immortality being inverted in keeping with the book's general emphasis on sickness and death. In chapter four of part one Miguel draws water from the well on Perico Montaña's estate after demeaning himself by «bailando en calzoncillos sobre la uva». Notwithstanding this indecorous display, Miguel reminds the company that in ancient Rome «las cubetas de los pozos ... ya fueron utilizadas con fines higiénicos por los mártires» (64). His remark seems incongruous at the time, yet it anticipates and glosses a crucial scene involving his *alter ego*, Joaquín, in chapter three of part two. Here Joaquín seeks desperately to cleanse his inner self by immersing his head in a bucket of water drawn from the well outside *la Damajuana* bar; as he drinks, «pensó de pronto que había un sapo en el fondo de la cubeta» (198). He is then summoned to go back inside and sing for the revellers, but he fails to perform to Don Gabriel's satisfaction and is dismissed. Outside in the *patio* «volvió a meter la cabeza dentro [de la cubeta] y bebía con la misma ansia que antes, pensando en el imaginario y gelatinoso reptar del sapo. El cante salía de la venta como un infecto reguero de saliva de sapo ... Y se volcó sobre el pilón, vomitando a violentas y convulsas tarascadas» (207). Polluting a communal water supply is a less than saintly act, but in Joaquín's mind the water is already contaminated at source, by the toad which may be taken to represent social evil. The apparent affront to standards of hygiene does not diminish his standing as a martyr; in fact, within the book's narrative structure Joaquín's involuntary pollution of the well precedes his death as did ritual ablution for early Christian martyrs.

Resonances of Classical mythology are also present in *Dos días de setiembre*. Miguel's irrational behaviour at the wine-pressing harks back to ancient rites:

> Dio un ridículo salto sobre uno de los montones de uvas, hundiéndose casi por completo en el pringoso y rezumante verdor... Se acercaron Carmela y el Cuba y, por fin, consiguieron levantarlo. A Miguel le chorreaba el zumo por la cara. Tenía los pantalones salpicados de manchas y hollejos. Aparentaba salir de un trance.
> —Bien, ya cumplí —dijo—. Ahora a beber. (60)

When he takes off his trousers and jumps into the press, «agarrándose torpemente al reborde de la madera podrida» (63), he dissolves into a group of «figuras de una absurda alegoría báquica» (62). The story of Bacchus/Dionysos does not in any way provide a running parallel to the action of *Dos días de setiembre,* but one of its details bears a telling resemblance to Joaquín's experience. Like Joaquín, Bacchus suffered imprisonment, at the hands of Pentheus of Thebes who is reputed to have been an unjust king. [35] Pressed to its furthest logical extreme, the analogy redounds to the discredit of the highest authority in Spain, indicting General Franco as the instigator of unjust imprisonments such as that of Joaquín in the «Penal del Puerto de Santa María» (102).

At the wine-pressing Miguel invokes the rite of Hercules and Geryon. Hercules killed this three-headed monster and stole his cattle in the tenth of his twelve labours. The story has considerable local relevance since, according to Pausanias, Geryon, King of Tartassus in Spain, was buried in the city of Gadeira (modern Cadiz) which became a centre of the ancient cult of Herakles. [36] But the most pointed significance of «el rito de Hércules y los Geriones» resides in the fact that it is supposed to «conjurar los maleficios de la tradición»: Miguel «cogió la jarra [de solera] y derramó un chorrito de vino sobre el terrizo» as a means of warding off danger (58). It is one of the novel's bitterest ironies that his gesture does nothing to alleviate the effects of a *damnosa hereditas* which hounds the community and claims its latest victim in Joaquín.

---

[35] See *The New Larousse Encyclopedia of Mythology* (London, 1973), 159.
[36] See ROBERT GRAVES, *The Greek Myths,* 2 vols. (Harmondsworth, 1977), II, 132-44.

Another element of ritual (associated, perhaps, with Hercules's capture of the Erymanthian Boar) [37] casts an ironic shadow over the action of Caballero Bonald's novel. In the course of an orgy of Dionysiac debauchery on Perico Montaña's estate, Miguel voices an absurd warning about a wild boar, telling his companions that «En las viñas, por si no lo sabíais, siempre anda suelto un jabalí cuando hay luna». He then proceeds to perform an eccentric ritual which, unbeknown to him, adumbrates Joaquín's death. Miguel interrupts the conversation a second time and exclaims: «¡El jabalí, el jabalí! ¡Sálvese quien pueda!» The narrative continues: «De las sombras del patio salió un perro canela, indeciso y cojeando de una pata. Miguel se adelantó para espantarlo. Se volvía con aire triunfante.» His confident boast that «Ya pasó el peligro, ha habido suerte» (55) matches his triumphal air, but it proves to be premature for, on the following night, his *alter ego* succumbs to the brutal force of death. It is this force which dog and boar represent. In a typically morbid scene, Joaquín's corpse attracts «dos perros que embestían y aullaban como lobos, venteando el hedor. Uno de los perros era cojo y de color canela» (283). Through this repetition a seemingly inconsequential detail comes to function as a thematic and structural motif in a text which moulds Classical mythology, Christian lore, collective psychology and historical analysis into a coherent symbolic projection of post-war Spain.

This reading of *Dos días de setiembre* prompts a reappraisal of the conventionally held view of it as «un prototípico libro social» [38] which marks the first stage in Caballero Bonald's evolution «de lo social a lo mítico». [39] *Dos días de setiembre* is in fact a hybrid text, at once social and mythical, which can only be forced into the narrow category of mimetic writing at the cost of ignoring its rich figurative texture. If Caballero Bonald's novel is to be categorised at all within the context of Spanish fiction in the 50s and 60s, then it belongs, surely, to the same grouping as *Con el viento solano* and *Gran Sol* by Ignacio Aldecoa, *Duelo en el paraíso* by Juan Goytisolo, and *El Jarama* by Rafael Sánchez Ferlosio. These are novels which capture the mood of post-war Spanish society through recourse to deliberately figurative strategies: they exploit Classical and Christian symbolism in the delineation of character and event (*Con el viento solano*, *Gran Sol* and *Duelo en el paraíso*), [40] they fashion symbolic landscapes in which the natural order

[37] See GRAVES, *The Greek Myths*, II, 113-16.
[38] SANTOS SANZ VILLANUEVA, *Historia de la novela social española (1942-75)*, II, 689.
[39] See CARMEN RUIZ BARRIONUEVO, «La obra narrativa de Caballero Bonald. De lo social a lo mítico», *Insula*, 396-97 (November-December 1979), p. 18.
[40] For a discussion of archetypal symbolism in the novels of Ignacio Aldecoa see the studies cited in notes 23 and 28 above. CURRIE K. THOMSON studies «The Dionysian Myth in Goytisolo's *Duelo en el paraíso*», *Symposium*, XXXV (1981-82), 341-56, and JO LABANYI argues against realist readings of the same novel, showing how Goytisolo mystifies the historical realities of the Spanish Civil War, in «The Ambiguous Implications of the Mythical References in Juan Goytisolo's *Duelo en el paraíso*», *MLR*, LXXX, 4 (October 1985), 845-57.

embodies destructive forces of history *(El Jarama),* and they focus on the suffering of individuals who are portrayed as the scapegoats of society (like Sebastián Vázquez in *Con el viento solano* and Lucita in *El Jarama).* [41] If it is true, as Ramón Buckley believes, that «cada coyuntura histórica exige una forma de novela», [42] then these novels together with *Dos días de setiembre* and others constitute a fictional paradigm in tune with the requirements of the age.

In chronological terms, *Dos días de setiembre* follows and elaborates on a type of novel established in the mid-1950s in Spain. Yet, as commentators unanimously agree, it is also a bridging text which anticipates developments in Spanish fiction generally associated with Luis Martín Santos and Juan Marsé. In Juan Carlos Curutchet's opinion, this applies above all in respect of the author's innovatory treatment of stylistic conventions. However, Caballero Bonald's vision of Spain as a body politic racked with disease and haunted by nightmares of violence is arguably a more important legacy. Other essays in this volume will consider the extent to which the thematic concerns of *Dos días de setiembre* surface in subsequent works of fiction; as a conclusion to this study we wish to note certain points of contact between Caballero Bonald's novel and the cinema.

A film by Federico Fellini features prominently in the penultimate chapter of *Dos días de setiembre* where Gloria and Tana, the daughters of Gabriel Varela and Felipe Gamero respectively, discuss *The Nights of Cabiria.* [43] The girls strongly disapprove because *The Nights of Cabiria* has «un argumento de lo más desagradable» about «una mujer de la vida que parece que no ha roto un plato y hay que ver»; the film's seedy atmosphere evinces a moralistic response from Gloria who complains that it is «Un asco, a mí que no me vengan con que eso es cine» (301). Caballero Bonald introduces these two censorious citizens partly as a means of satirising the narrow-minded puritanical attitudes of the local bourgeoisie, and principally in order to define an aesthetic credo valid for his novel which matches the sordidness of Fellini's film in its uncompromising presentation of the themes of alcoholism, prostitution (in the character of Encarna), suicide and sickness, thus falling readily into the category of narratives which are «del estilo de la Cabiria esa» (302).

In the course of their conversation Gloria and Tana agree that they would rather see «una comedia americana» which, in the context, seems to typify a facile and escapist art. Their preference for American entertainment

---

[41] See FRANCISCO GARCÍA SARRIÁ's interpretation of the role of Lucita, in «*El Jarama.* Muerte y merienda de Lucita», cited in 7 above.

[42] RAMÓN BUCKLEY, *Problemas formales en la novela española contemporánea,* second edition (Barcelona, 1973), p. 74.

[43] *Le notti di Cabiria* was made in 1956 and starred Giulietta Masina as the prostitute, Gelsomina Cabiria. The film has been studied by ANDRÉ BAZIN, «Cabiria: The Voyage to the End of Neorealism», in *Federico Fellini. Essays in Criticism,* ed. PETER BONDANELLA (Oxford, 1978), pp. 94-102.

is not, however, innocent of political implications, since it denotes support for the cultural order of Francoism (Legislation of 1944 imposed restrictions on the number of domestic films screened in Spanish cinemas and encouraged the showing of countless anodyne foreign productions), [44] and betokens acceptance of the North American presence on Spanish soil as determined by the military and economic agreements of 1953 which authorised the establishment of American military bases on sites such as Torrejón de Ardoz in the province of Madrid and Rota on the Gulf of Cadiz. The young Madrilenian protagonists of Sánchez Ferlosio's *El Jarama* find the proximity of Torrejón unnerving; the author of *Dos días de setiembre* likewise examines the influence of the base at Rota on local community values. In the storyline, Gloria secures a secretarial position at «La Base» (297) and is promised a salary which throws into stark relief the relative poverty of the society in which she lives: she tells Tana that her monthly income will be higher than that of a qualified doctor (299). Through the inclusion of this comment Caballero Bonald demonstrates the disruptive effect of the American intrusion treated comically in Luis G. Berlanga's *Bienvenido Míster Marshall* (1952), and, more pointedly, he turns Gloria's indignant remarks about the «mujer de la vida» in Fellini's film against her, by insinuating that her acceptance of a disproportionately high salary is no less professional a form of prostitution. Here the worlds of film and fiction intersect in an instructive *mise en abîme*.

Very interestingly, there are striking resemblances in this respect between *Dos días de setiembre* and Carlos Saura's film, *La caza* (1965). Latent violence, suspicion and resentment, coupled with a destructive sexual urge and death instinct, characterise the social groups depicted in both works. The moral shortcomings of Caballero Bonald's characters reappear in Saura's microcosmic picture of post-war Spanish society, where they are accompanied by similar images of sickness: José takes tablets to ease the lingering pain caused by a war-wound (cf. Don Gabriel who carries with him «un diminuto tubo de pastillas» in *Dos días de setiembre*, p. 86); Luis imagines the hunting party to be infected with mixamatosis, just as Rafael «se imaginaba que [Julián Cobeña] debía tener todo el cuerpo atacado por el hongo del mildiu» which threatens to destroy the vines at Valdecañizo (169). Luis's «borracheras de coñac» mirror the alcoholic excesses of several characters in Caballero Bonald's novel, and awaken in him a perverse instinct for cruelty. In *La caza* the effects of the Spanish Civil War on the mind of the nation are shown to persist with the same damaging force as in *Dos días de setiembre*. As the hunters relax after lunch, they hear a voice on the radio saying «He soñado esta noche, Papá... A mí me mataban con perros.» Both sets

---

[44] In the opinion of the Marxist critic, Domènec Font, an inevitable — and ironic — consequence of State legislation relating to the cinema in the 1940s was the «colonization» of Spanish markets by American monopoly interests. See FONT, *Del azul al verde. El cine español durante el franquismo* (Barcelona, 1976), pp. 44-47.

of characters are bedevilled by spectres of the past: José uncovers a skeleton which one of his companions identifies as «un muerto de la guerra que tiene escondido»; in *Dos días de setiembre,* Miguel jabbers incoherently about «los muertos sin enterrar» in his family (60). Saura's hunters are haunted by the memory of Arturo who «se suicidó» (cf. the *arrumbador* whose story is told on p. 222 of the novel). The film's barren landscape pitted with rabbit holes reminds one of the protagonists of a site where mass executions took place in the Civil War, and the sweltering atmosphere consolidates a climate of impending violence, as in *Dos días de setiembre.* Finally, although mythical underpinnings are more easily detected in the novel than in the film, the imposition of a deformed foot on Juan, who lives among animals on a deserted farm, points to a possible association with Oedipus who was abandoned at birth on Mount Cithaeron with his feet pierced and bound together (hence the literal meaning of his name in ancient Greek: Oedipus = «swell-foot»). [45] The detail is one which evokes a mythical order of ominous monstrosity and ritual blood-letting totally consonant with the mood and outcome of the film.

Quite clearly, many of the themes, descriptive motifs and aspects of design in *La caza* have their immediate origins in *Dos días de setiembre.* Caballero Bonald's novel may thus be seen to occupy a central position in a cultural continuum which comprises not only modes of writing (from neo-realism, exemplified by Aldecoa and Sánchez Ferlosio, to critical or dialectical realism, illustrated in the work of Martín Santos, the evolved Juan Goytisolo and Juan Marsé), but also visual forms of expression extending from cinematic neo-realism, as practised by José Antonio Nieves Conde in *Surcos* (1951), to the more idiosyncratic style adopted by Saura in films like *La caza* and *Ana y los lobos* which substitute figurative procedures, including those of allegory, for a naive representational aesthetic. Embedded in a historical conjuncture when changes were beginning to occur in the social and economic orders of Franco's Spain, *Dos días de setiembre* exemplifies a young generation's search for artistic forms and strategies sufficiently mature and flexible to mediate a complex vision of the nation's past and present.

---

[45] The symbolic significance of Oedipus's name is a crucial part of CLAUDE LEVI-STRAUSS's interpretation of the myth of Oedipus. See his *Structural Anthropology,* trans. Claire Jacobson and Brooke Grundfest Schoepf (Harmondsworth, 1972), pp. 213-18.

2

TIEMPO DE SILENCIO: «LOS ESPAÑOLES PINTADOS POR SÍ MISMOS»

In the history of contemporary Spanish literature no single title has impressed itself so deeply on the critical mind as *Tiempo de silencio* by Luis Martín Santos. A voluminous bibliography attests to the remarkable conceptual density and technical sophistication of this novel which lends itself accommodatingly to a wide variety of theoretical approaches. One group of commentators stresses Luis Martín Santos's interest in existential themes and notes how he embodies certain key concepts in his novel at the levels of character and plot; recent exponents of this method include Alfonso Rey and John Lyon. [1] A second school of critics documents the presence in *Tiempo de silencio* of mythical material drawn from Classical sources; the myths of Odysseus and Orpheus, among others, provide often ironic parallels to the action of *Tiempo de silencio,* filling it with archetypal resonances. [2] A third approach regards *Tiempo de silencio* as an allegory of social and political conditions in Franco's Spain; in one of a number of articles which discuss the imagery of disease in the book Gustavo Pérez Firmat illustrates the author's use of the cancer motif to denote sickness in the body politic of Spain. [3] A fourth approach derives from psychoanalytic theory: Martín San-

---

[1] ALFONSO REY, *Construcción y sentido de Tiempo de silencio* (Madrid, 1977); JOHN LYON, «Don Pedro's Complicity: an Existential Dimension of *Tiempo de silencio*», *MLR*, LXXIV (1979), 69-78. These authors elaborate on the conclusions of SHERMANN EOFF and JOSÉ SCHRAIBMAN, «Dos novelas del absurdo: *L'Etranger* y *Tiempo de silencio*», *Papeles de Son Armadans*, LVI (1970), 213-41, and on those of GEMMA ROBERTS, *Temas existenciales en la novela española de postguerra* (Madrid, 1973), pp. 129-203.

[2] Martín Santos's use of mythical material has been considered by JULIAN PALLEY, «The Periplus of Don Pedro», *BHS*, XLVIII (1971), 239-54, RICARDO GULLÓN, «Mitos órficos y cáncer social», *El Urogallo*, 17 (1972), pp. 80-89, and JUAN VILLEGAS, *La estructura mítica del héroe* (Barcelona, 1973), pp. 203-30. See also JEAN TENA, «*Tiempo de silencio* comme mythologie», in *Deux romans de la rupture?* (Toulouse-le-Mirail, 1980), pp. 31-39.

[3] GUSTAVO PÉREZ FIRMAT, «Repetition and Excess in *Tiempo de silencio*», *PMLA*, XCVI (1981), 194-209. An allegorical reading was first proposed by JUAN CARLOS CURUTCHET in his pioneering study, «Luis Martín Santos: el fundador», first published in *Cuadernos de Ruedo Ibérico*, nos. 17 & 18 (1968), pp. 3-18 and 3-15 respectively, and

Oedipus complex stressed in this fi...

tos's own study entitled *Libertad, temporalidad y transferencia en el psicoanálisis existencial*[4] serves as a starting point for readings of his novel which describes a classic case of Oedipal anxiety in the individual figure of Pedro.[5] A recent study acknowledges that the Oedipal model may also be applied to the community of relations depicted in *Tiempo de silencio*. In the view of Claude Talahite, Martín Santos's novel «met en scène, aussi bien sur le mode réaliste ... que sur le mode symbolique ... le meurtre des fils par les pères et une société qui se stérilise»; here the psychoanalytic method combines with ideological considerations to broaden our understanding of the text.[6]

...ecded que le existencia dan bien en el fin Florita's sister - F & D death old woman, m... prostitutes una sociedad sin magu...

The value of a plural reading of *Tiempo de silencio* is demonstrated in two other studies. Emilio Díaz Valcárcel has sought to uncover significant relations between elements of myth, social criticism and ideology in *Tiempo de silencio*. Following the «genetic structural» method of Lucien Goldmann, Díaz Valcárcel attempts, with sporadic success, to «profundizar semánticamente en enunciados que, a primera vista, parecen inocentes de toda carga ideológica».[7] A more ambitious and comprehensive study is Jo Labanyi's reading of *Tiempo de silencio,* where this critic adopts a multiple perspective incorporating existential psychoanalysis after Sartre, variations on Freudian psychology, the ideological concerns of Erich Fromm, and theories of irony.[8] Ms. Labanyi's account and other current interpretations of Martín Santos's novel reveal a welcome tendency to synthesize earlier univocal readings, and thereby to do greater justice to the complexity of *Tiempo de silencio*. It is our intention to build on existing strengths of the critical tradition in an attempt to enhance appreciation of that quality of unity within diversity which distinguishes Martín Santos's novel. The author's interests in psychol-

---

reprinted in *Cuatro ensayos sobre la nueva novela española* (Montevideo, 1973), pp. 29-69 (pp. 35-37), and by José Schraibman, «La novela española contemporánea», *RHM*, XXXV (1969), 113-21 (p. 119).

[4] Luis Martín Santos, *Libertad, temporalidad y transferencia en el psicoanálisis existencial* (Barcelona, 1964).

[5] See the readings of Carlos Feal Deibe, «Consideraciones psicoanalíticas sobre *Tiempo de silencio* de Luis Martín Santos», *RHM*, XXXVI (1970-71), 118-27, Walter Holzinger «*Tiempo de silencio*: an Analysis», *RHM*, XXXVII (1972-73), 73-90, and José Schraibman, «*Tiempo de silencio* y el psicoanálisis existencial», *Hispanófila*, 62 (January 1978), 109-17.

[6] Claude Talahite, «*Tiempo de silencio*: une écriture de silence», in *Luis Martín Santos. Tiempo de silencio* (Montpellier, 1980), p. 8. Jean Alsina observes accurately that «L'analyse sémiotique de *Tiempo de silencio* par Claude Talahite débouche parfaitement ... sur une lecture politique», in *Deux romans de la rupture?* (Toulouse-le-Mirail, 1980), p. 146. José Schraibman's note, «*Tiempo de silencio* y la cura psiquiátrica de un pueblo: España», *Ínsula*, 365 (April 1977), p. 3, fails to develop the idea that Martín Santos delves into the collective soul of the nation.

[7] Emilio Díaz Valcárcel, *La visión del mundo en la novela (Tiempo de silencio, de Luis Martín Santos)* (Río Piedras, Puerto Rico, 1982), p. 92.

[8] Jo Labanyi, *Ironía e historia en Tiempo de silencio* (Madrid, 1985). A paper based on an extract from this study was delivered to an audience of the Association of Hispanists of Great Britain and Ireland when it met in March 1984 in Exeter (England).

ogy and sexuality, medicine, the history and institutions of Spain, and the nature of art provide a framework for our reading of *Tiempo de silencio*.

Martín Santos's psychoanalytical bias surfaces most spectacularly in that fragment of *Tiempo de silencio* which recounts the episode of Pedro's visit to the cabaret with Dorita and her mother. At the start the cabaret is identified as a ritual setting conducive to «el ensueño, la alucinación mescalínica, el inconsciente colectivo». In this atmosphere spectators temporarily suspend all rationality and surrender to the allure of the unconscious which manifests itself primarily in the form of «el arquetipo de lo que deseamos desde la cama solitaria de los trece años de edad» (219). [9] The archetype of the opposite sex is thus held to exercise fascination, to confirm a person's sexual identity and to constitute his or her psychic integrity. It is significant that such archetypes originate not at some subconscious level in the mind of the individual but in the collective unconscious: echoing the theories of Carl Gustav Jung, Martín Santos explains that an archetype is an «entidad ... esencial que ya no en los cuerpos grácilmente agitados se contiene, sino en la propia alma avariciosa de quien como a signos de una escritura fácilmente comprendida —desde antes de haber nacido cada individuo—, por la especie los mira» (220). [10] Archetypes, then, are projections of a people's collective spiritual needs and normative expectations. In the setting of the cabaret both male and female spectators «se proyectan sobre el escenario» (221), a stage which is both a literal referent and a symbolic «espacio desnudado» in which «el buen pueblo acumulado, sentado, apretado, sudante, oprimiente-oprimido» (222) experiences exhilaration, consolation and the sublimation of its primitive urges (225).

The analogy which the narrator draws between a dramatic performance and the «signos de una escritura fácilmente comprendida» teasingly invites the reader of *Tiempo de silencio* to consider the role of archetypal images, particularly those of human types, in literature. In the cabaret episode of his novel Martín Santos gives an illustration in the person of the «supervedette máxima» who is «la imagen policromada de la mujer» (222). «Con su nueva virginidad cotinocturna envuelta en transparentes peplos» (219), this artiste represents the type of «la hurí lasciva» (148); «cubierta toda ella de papel de plata o escamas de pez» (221), she is also a materialisation of the siren «con su cola asombrosa de pez hembra» which Pedro had drawn earlier on the wall of his prison cell (86). Her function in the cabaret is to proclaim seductively a «mensaje de alegría, de paz y de concordia secular» which stands in an ambiguous relation to historical reality. Through a re-enactment of the sexual conquests of Eugenia de Montijo, the courtesan who won the heart of Charles Louis Napoleon and became Empress of France

[9] Reference will be made throughout to the ninth edition of *Tiempo de silencio*, published by Seix Barral (Barcelona, 1971).

[10] See CARL GUSTAV JUNG, *The Archetypes and the Collective Unconscious*, second edition (London, 1971), pp. 3-72.

from 1853 to 1871, this queen of the stage «[hace] sentirse vengado al vencido pueblo» which, in 1808, had been ravaged by the invading forces of Napoleon I, Charles Louis's uncle. The singer's «triunfal entronización» is thus «materia de consolación» (223) since it facilitates the release of deeply entrenched popular resentment against the French. No less important is the fact that her performance, like that of Amparito Rivelles in the title role of José López Rubio's film, *Eugenia de Montijo* (1944), serves the ideological aims of the Franco régime, because it reinforces the people's alienation and complicity in their own repression. «Supervedette», chorus and spectators are all led to «olvi[dar] sus enajenaciones» by participating in «una euforia incesante que a la mala alimentación sustituyera» (220). Through this brilliant exercise in the psychoanalysis of a collective subject Martín Santos reveals the hidden connections between sexuality and power, and illustrates the ideological use to which certain archetypal images may be put.

Tiempo de silencio features many examples of this practice. Pedro recalls «la teoría alegórica en que la lujuria es una mujer desnuda con una manzana en la mano y la soberbia una mujer vestida con una corona en la cabeza» (139), and thereby documents a traditional tendency in Western art to exploit images of women for sexist and moralistic purposes. A typical archetype is the woman who preys on men. Matías incorporates this misogynistic image into his thoughts on Pedro's loss of freedom following his seduction by, not of, Dorita: «Osado el que penetra en la carne femenina, ¿cómo podrá permanecer entero tras la cópula? Vagina dentata, castración afectiva, emasculación posesiva, mío, mío, tú eres mío» (161). In metaphorical terms reminiscent of the cabaret episode Matías voyeuristically imagines Dorita's sexual performance to have been as consummate as that of any actress: «Ríase usted de la Sarah Bernhardt. Qué escenita. Te amo, te como, te devoro, te hundo los colmillos en la víscera más tierna. Y yo espectador privilegiado en proscenio especial, representación privatissime» (162). Ironically, the image of the «devoradora de hombres»[11] does not represent Pedro's ideal woman who is «otra clase de mujer, de la que lo importante no será ya la exuberancia elemental y cíclica, sino la lucidez libre y decidida» (95). That type is absent from the dramatis personae of *Tiempo de silencio* which nevertheless displays a varied repertoire of conventional images of men and women.

Women characters including Dorita's grandmother, Doña Luisa —«la severa matrona» of the brothel (150)— and Encarna/Ricarda, el Muecas's wife, are cast in archetypal moulds of the literary and pictorial tradition of the West. Dorita's anonymous grandmother is an up-to-date version of an age-old antecedent: «La celestina que es celestina para no morir de ham-

---

[11] Doña Bárbara is described as «la devoradora de hombres» in chapter three of part one of RÓMULO GALLEGOS's novel. Gallegos's use of this sexist image betrays the ideological prejudices of his class.

bre o para no tener que quitar los visillos de sus ventanas.» Characterised as «la femineidad vuelta astucia», she is fired by post-menopausal sexual frustration and a thirst for revenge on the opposite sex. She seeks «¡Venganza contra el repugnante protervo bailarín hembra [who seduced her daughter]! ¡Desquite contra el banquero grueso con sus gafas, astuto catador de mercancías!» (97). A widow, she is introduced in the fourth fragment of the novel as «una anciana de natural monárquico y legitimista [quien] a pesar de su edad era ordeno y mando» (36). The profile outlined here clearly identifies her as a matriarch who, in the manner of Lorca's Bernarda Alba, embodies the principle of authority and the rule of law.

Part stereotype and part caricature, this character in turn projects a stereotyped image of the male. Of her dead husband she reminisces «¡Ese sí que era hombre!» (80), and asserts that «Un hombre se tiene que foguear como los soldados». Her unrestrained glorification of man-the-warrior explains in large measure her underlying contempt for Pedro who, she thinks, «es como nuestro San Luis Gonzaga, que no le faltan más que el rosario y los lirios». As James Joyce informs his readers in section I of *A Portrait of the Artist as a Young Man,* Aloysius Gonzaga figures as one of «three patrons of holy youth» and sexual innocence. [12] Manifestly virgin (lily-white) and an example of acute Oedipal anxiety, Pedro falls lamentably short of the standard of virility demanded of him by his *patrona.* «Es lo que les pasa a los hombres de ahora», she tells him:

> No llegaron a tiempo a la última guerra y con tanta paz y la alimentación floja que han tenido en la infancia, están poco seguros de lo que es una mujer y creen que es como un diamante que hay que coger con pinzas y que hay que hablar con ella antes en francés para averiguar lo que tiene dentro. Si hubieran estado en avances, conquistas y violaciones y aprendieran así bien lo del botín y el sagrado derecho a la rapiña de los pueblos conquistados y no lo hubieran leído sólo en novelas, otro gallo les cantara. (81)

The difference between Pedro and her husband, «lleno para mí de encanto, con sus grandes bigotes y sus ojos oscuros y su marcialidad esquiva» (17), is accentuated by an implicit contrast between San Luis Gonzaga and the more memorable San Lorenzo who was martyred by the Romans. On the final page of *Tiempo de silencio* Pedro acknowledges that «sanlorenzo era un macho, no gritaba, no gritaba, estaba en silencio mientras lo tostaban torquemadas paganos» (240), fully aware that he does not match the type.

Martín Santos brings into play another of the stereotyped images of man fabricated by the collective mind: that of the primitive hunter possessed of «el poder viril del macho». At the verbena which he attends with Dorita and her mother Pedro tries his hand at the shooting range, to the undisguised

---

[12] JAMES JOYCE, *A Portrait of the Artist as a Young Man* (Harmondsworth, 1967), p. 56.

amusement of the narrator who remarks that «tirando sobre un blanco...
se puede cumplir, con más modestia, la misma función erótico-sexual que
cazando un antílope en el África negra con el fin de que nuestra ausente-
presente hembra pueda admirar el trofeo un día». Exposed as a hunter
manqué, Pedro then proceeds «al sitio donde se pega con un martillo muy
pesado y una pieza de hierro sube por una especie de carril hasta que
llega arriba y si llega arriba del todo da —clin— y se enciende una
luz» (230). In this second test of strength he is proven unmanly and inferior
to the primitive Cartucho who «con sólo una mano izquierda y un rápido
reviramiento de cuerpo ágil encendía la luz roja como un aviso de alar-
ma» (231).

Allied to the type of the hunter is that of the bullfighter, quintessentially
Spanish and perceived conventionally as popular, heroic and virile. [13] Alfonso Rey has elucidated Martín Santos's treatment of the subject and imagery of bullfighting in *Tiempo de silencio;* [14] of particular interest is the
debasement of the bullfighter type in the outrageous figure of the «torero-
bailarín-marica» (22). «El protervo», as he is venomously remembered, dis-
honoured Dorita's mother and abandoned her for the company of friends
who were «todos de su estilo como medio hembras también, pequeñitos ...
y hablaban andaluz y batían palmas muy bien» (23). In this portrait Martín
Santos implements his own injunction to deconstruct myths of «la España
de pandereta», thus anticipating Carlos Saura's less virulent but equally
systematic debunking of the national types of «majas y toreros» (182) in
his film, *Carmen* (see below, pp. 87-90).

A parodic intent is also visible in Martín Santos's presentation of el
Muecas. This character ekes out a livelihood for himself and his three
dependents by scavenging in local refuse tips and exploiting the waste land
around his shanty hovel. Like Dorita's grandmother and her servant, «la
maritornes ceñuda» (116), el Muecas is modelled on a famous literary antecedent. «Gentleman-farmer Muecasthone» (56) is elevated to the rank of
«terrateniente» (50) and masquerades as a shepherd: «Pastor, que iba hacia
su cura de almas, informaba del ambiente espiritual de su poblado» (56).
His biblical aura is enhanced in the description of him as «patriarca bíbli-
co» (55). Yet, el Muecas is the antithesis of the Good Shepherd celebrated
in Christian scripture. He represents authority and property ownership,
principles which he upholds through the exercise of brutal violence and

---

[13] In *Sangre y arena* (Valencia, 1908) Vicente Blasco Ibáñez portrays a *matador*,
Juan Gallardo, who for some time enjoys massive popular adulation befitting his type.
A quarter of a century later, Federico García Lorca attributes exemplary qualities of
heroism, beauty and majesty to the bullfighter whose death he mourns in «Llanto por
Ignacio Sánchez Mejías». For a less heroic but no less telling view of the virile *torero*,
see the graphic description of Leopold Bloom's «erotic photocard» which depicts «buccal
coition between nude señorita (rere presentation, superior position) and nude torero
(fore presentation, inferior position)», in *Ulysses* (Harmondsworth, 1969), p. 642.
[14] Alfonso Rey, *Construcción y sentido de Tiempo de silencio*, pp. 205-15.

sexual abuse. Amador informs Pedro that el Muecas «es muy burro. Es exactamente un animal. Y siempre con la navaja encima a todas partes» (33). In short, he is the prototype of the phallocentric male. In courtship he «violó con dolor a su mujer» (202), and on the immediate plane of the narrative he indulges in incestuous relations with his daughters which result in a pregnancy, a barbaric abortion and the death of Florita from an unstaunched haemorrhage.

El Muecas is the personification of «El macho cabrío» as painted by Goya: «El gran buco en el esplendor de su gloria, en la prepotencia del dominio, en el usufructo de la adoración centrípeta. En el que el cuerno no es cuerno ominoso, sino signo de glorioso dominio fálico.» Martín Santos gives the following commentary on Goya's painting which is entitled *Escena de brujas* (see Plate 2):

> El gran buco... mi[ra] a la muchedumbre femelle que yace sobre su regazo en ademán de auparishtaka y de las que los abortos vivos parecen expresar en súplica sincera la posible revitalización por el contacto de quien... se complace en depositar la pezuña izquierda benevolentemente sobre el todavía no frío ya escuálido, no suficientemente alimentado cuerpo del raquitismus enclencorum de las mauvaises couches reduplicativas, de las que las resultantes momificadas penden colgadas a intervalos regulares de un vástago flexible. (127)

Laced with black humour, this verbal *tour de force* superimposes on the canvas disturbingly exact images of el Muecas's abuse of the dying Florita and of her protesting sister whom he knocks to the ground and silences with a flurry of «ciegas patadas» (114).

The novel boasts several other illustrations of phallocentrism. Most notable among these is Cartucho, who «paseaba con una mano tocándose la navaja cabritera y con la otra la hombría que se le enfriaba». The mysterious movements of people in and around his girl friend Florita's home arouse Cartucho's suspicions and make the forceful use of at least one of these instruments inevitable. «Como lo vea a quien que sea lo pincho», he threatens (105). Amador, «seguro de su sexo» (28), is equally potent and does questionable honour to his «nombre de hombre fatal» (236) within and outside the confines of marriage. And the guard of the train which transports Pedro to provincial obscurity is perceived predictably as «el hombre fálico de la gorra roja terminada en punto de cilindro rojo con su fecundidad inagotable para la producción de movimientos rectilíneos». Pedro admits that a contrast with this man is singularly unflattering: «Ahí se está paseando orgulloso de su gran prepucio rojo-cefálico, con su pito enrollado, dotado de múltiples atributos que desencadenarán la marcha erecta del órgano gigante que se clavará en el vientre de las montañas mientras yo me estoy dejando capar» (237). A variant of the discredited type under consideration here is Doña Luisa, the brothel madame, who is invested with «el aspecto providente y confidencial de gran madre fálica» (151). «Hormigareina» of a distorted world which is at once an «hormiguero» and a «palacio de las hijas de la noche» (147), she, like Dorita's grandmother and the female character, Gorgo, who appropriates Bion's beard in *El adefesio* by Rafael Alberti, usurps the role of *paterfamilias* generally reserved for dominant males in society at large.

The principles of «ordeno y mando» and «dominio fálico» are located by Martín Santos within the institutions of the family and its counterpart, marriage. The disorientated protagonist of *Tiempo de silencio* anticipates the time when he will have to comply with «obligaciones ineludibles», «como hombre de honor inspirado para la defensa de la familia y del status actualis situationis» (99). In the cabaret sequence the narrator argues, tongue-in-cheek, that «El amor del pueblo ... no es amor prostituido, sino amor matrimoniable, instituido sobre antiquísimas instituciones, bendecido por el necesario número de varones tonsurados y expuesto como ejemplo de coincidencia y de decoro, de equilibrio y paz no conturbada» (222-23). This statement asserts the interdependence of Church, family and the State in the monolith of Franco's Spain. At the same time, mischievous play on the words «prostituido» and «instituido» points subversively to the failure of institutional attempts to harmonise the requirements of instinct and society.

Tiempo de silencio subjects the institutions of marriage and the family to a remorseless critique. «La familia muequil», comprising «el ciudadano Muecas bien establecido» (58), «sus dos hijas núbiles», and «la mole mansa y muda de la esposa» (54) who wears «una alianza matrimonial que carece de todo significado», is the *contraimagen* of the ideal family unit. Husband and wife share «el mismo ancho camastro con hijos ya crecidos a los que nada puede quedar oculto», a state of affairs which implies an affront to human dignity and an assault on all «valores espirituales» (43); the family's spiritual plight is reflected in the physical squalor of «los soberbios alcázares de la miseria» which they inhabit (42). In the story line of *Tiempo de silencio* el Muecas augments the family's income by obliging his daughters to incubate cancer-bearing mice, which he has stolen from the research institute where Pedro and Amador work, in small pouches hung around their necks, thus ensuring a continuous supply of mice for re-sale to the laboratory. At first, the reader cannot deny el Muecas a certain grudging respect for the resourcefulness he shows in adversity, but a more reasoned response lays bare the full implications of the scavenger's actions. At an allegorical level, the introduction of a strain of mice «de la cepa illinoica» (11) into the home connotes the acceptance of American economic aid under the agreements of 1951 and 1953 by the Spanish Head of State whose authority is caricatured in the figure of el Muecas. And, at another, symbolic, level of interpretation, the same action signifies the pollution of the family since the creatures which el Muecas brings into the home belong to «una raza de ratones cancerígenos degenerada» (29). These symbolic overtones are confirmed by the experience of another family. Dorita's grandfather had fought in the «campaña de Filipinas» and returned home «inútil para la fecundación» (18) on account of a venereal infection contracted from «una tagala». «La esterilidad vergonzante del viejo coronel» (180) effectively frustrated the hopes of his wife who still ruminates «A mí que me hubiera gustado tener tres o cuatro [críos]» (18). As in the former instance, a father figure is responsible for introducing sickness —cancer, syphilis, sterility— into the body of the family.

It is surely no accident that two «matrimonios sin hijos» (22) figure among the former inmates of the *pensión* which Dorita's grandmother runs; the house stands out clearly as a microcosm of sterility. Further examination of *Tiempo de silencio* reveals a widespread pattern of sexual sickness within families. Amador's marriage has produced no off-spring; in the terms of one of Martín Santos's many synecdoches, his wife is a «vientre sin hijos, todavía concupiscente» (156). Matías's family is ridden with cancer. The guests at the party which his mother organises gossip about his aptly-named aunt Dolores, and glibly diagnose breast cancer: «¿Para qué lo va a negar usted? Es cosa sabida. Cáncer de pecho.» The heartless speaker then points out that «Todas mueren de eso en la familia ... Ya se sabe que su madre tuvo cáncer y su hermana, la monja, cáncer ...». The paragraph containing these pregnant statements concludes with some considerations «acerca de los derechos de las mujeres en el matrimonio cuando no se ha firmado en su día el contrato de separación de bienes» (138), thus linking cancer with the legal institution of marriage and putting forward a thesis, that marriage and the family are unstable, unhealthy institutions which may have fatal consequences for women.

Existing criticism of the novel recognises the importance of images of sickness and vivisection to Luis Martín Santos's argument. Like Pedro in the opening sequence of the book, he is peering, under laboratory conditions and with microscopic vision, at cancerous cells —«mitosis anormales»— in the body politic of Spain. «El terebrante husmeador de la realidad viva» who wields a «ceñido escalpelo que penetra en lo que se agita y descubre allí algo que nunca vieron ojos no ibéricos» (7-8), is the author himself. The motif of the penetrating scalpel is borrowed from the prologue of *Abel Sánchez* by Miguel de Unamuno who, admitting the fact that «El público no gusta que se le llegue con el escalpelo a hediondas simas del alma humana», defiantly proceeded in that text to dissect the substance of «la lepra nacional española». [15] Martín Santos is equally tenacious and explicit and, certainly, more precise in the historical detail of his vision. A symptom of the disease which he identifies in the tissue of the body of Spain is war. Dorita's grandmother laments, in an early conversation with Pedro, that «Usted es tan niño que no ha tenido que ir a ninguna guerra». Pedro replies with characteristic diffidence that «Desgraciadamente yo soy pacífico. No me interesan más

[15] MIGUEL DE UNAMUNO, *Abel Sánchez,* fourteenth edition (Madrid, 1979), pp. 10-11.

luchas que las de los virus con los anticuerpos» (39). The entire exchange evokes inescapably the Spanish Civil War. The image of «las falanges de la ciencia» in which Pedro is a low-ranking officer reinforces the idea. An ironic narrator reflects on the «multitud estudiosa e investigante» which resembles «un ejército aguerrido, llevando al brazo no armas destructoras, no bayonetas relampagueantes, sino microscopios, teodolitos, reglas de cálculo y pipetas capilares [marchando] en grandes pelotones bien organizados» (207).

What existing interpretations of Martín Santos's novel have failed to note is the correlation between sickness, the experience of women and the family in *Tiempo de silencio*. Our analysis of these conceptual elements prompts the conclusion that, at one level, the book presents an allegorical picture of the family of Spain. The country is depicted as an organic community harbouring apparently hereditary diseases which are spread across virtually the entire class spectrum, reaching into every national institution and affecting women—mothers, daughters, grandmothers, wives and aunts— in a particularly insidious way. The upper echelons of Spanish society are represented here by Matías's family in which «Todas mueren [de cáncer]» (138); Dorita's sterile family represents the lower middle class, that of Amador a still lower-level social order; «el bajo pueblo y la masa indocta» indulge «las funciones más bajas de la naturaleza humana», but at the risk of requiring «lavados con permanganato» administered by specialists in the treatment of anti-social diseases: «Fimosis, Sífilis, Venéreo» (30-31).

A roll-call of the characters who are afflicted by sickness highlights Luis Martín Santos's systematic strategy of defaming the principal institutions of Spain. The list includes a nun (representing the Holy Orders and, by extension, the Church) who died of cancer; a colonel (the Armed Forces) who contracted syphilis while fighting in a colonial war; as many as two childless «matrimonios de funcionarios del Ministerio de la Gobernación» in Madrid (the seat of national government) (22); a police officer who, in the course of his interrogation of Pedro, remarks that «Mi madre murió de cáncer» (196); a second police officer, Similiano, who suffers internal disorders and aspires to being transferred to the Mediterranean coast «para poder tomar el sol directamente en la tripa como decía aquel doctor que fue el único que me entendió. Todo el día tomando el sol en la tripa y seguro que se acababan los retortijoncillos y los hazmerreíres hidro-aéreos» (160). To this list may be added a final item which stands for all Institutions writ large with initial capital letters. «Los Institutos, los Consejos, las doctas Corporaciones, las venerables Casas matrices» (206-07) are denoted metonymically by the cancer research institute from which Pedro is expelled —or aborted— before the completion of his project. In the symbolic idiom of the book these «Casas matrices» house disease and, by virtue of the substantive epithet, are especially vulnerable to cancer of the womb.

Martín Santos's choice of an apparently hereditary «cáncer inguinal» as the subject of Pedro's research, and the particular prominence given in the novel to cancer of the womb (Spanish «matriz»), highlight once more the role of women in his symbolic critique of the family of Spain. His vivisection of the nation's body politic reveals the vulnerability of a woman's position in society, particularly in the face of the law. The topic of the «separación de bienes» in a broken marriage, which is located tellingly in the context of a discussion about fatal breast cancer (138), is further elaborated in Pedro's tortuous final monologue. Imagining the life that awaits him in the provinces, Pedro looks forward to eating «ancas de rana», an animal which he has hitherto only encountered on the dissecting table of the research laboratory. The crucial point is that he perceives in the fate of frogs an emblem of woman's subjugation. In fact he links vivisection to a famous movement of early twentieth-century social reform, observing that «Esto es, la vivisección, las sufragistas inglesas protestando, igual exactamente, igual que si fuera eso, la vivisección» (235). According to this image women are treated no better than animals in Spanish society, being subjected to the rigours of the (phallic) knife *in vivo;* their status as objects of the author's probing analysis is also vividly expressed by the analogy.

Our reading up to this point captures faithfully the pessimistic implications of Martín Santos's symbolic dissection of «la realidad viva» of Spain. However, there exists one unit, or cell, within the prolific family of the nation which is free of the effects of «el fenómeno que sume a las familias humanas en la desolación» (12). That is el Muecas's family which, unlike Dorita's or Cartucho's, comprises two children and both parents. [16] On the one hand, el Muecas's family is the most offensive example of phallic abuse contained in the book; under his tutelage, three women endure poverty and degradation; the death of Florita in barbaric circumstances is an event of the purest pathos. Yet, on the other hand, the family provides an illustration of effective and, indeed, miraculous survival in a sub-human environment. It is evident that Florita is ultimately a victim, not of environmental conditions, but of her father's instinctive brutality and Pedro's ineptitude. Prior to the tragic night of her death she had enjoyed immunity to contagion by disease. Amador offers Pedro the intriguing explanation that «Lo que pasa es que, a los pobres, nada se les contagia. Están ya inmunizados con tanta porquería» (35).

The untainted members of el Muecas's family are all female. The key figures in this respect are Florita and her mother to whom she is linked by the symbol of the earth. Encarna/Ricarda may be «treated like dirt» by her husband, the «terrateniente», but she is exalted by the author as an archetypal earth mother and identified as a «ser de tierra» (201) who voluntarily descends into the bowels of the earth to rescue Pedro from his «subterránea

---

[16] CLAUDE TALAHITE observes that «Il n'y a pas de père parmi les acteurs du récit, à l'exception de Muecas», in «*Tiempo de silencio:* une écriture de silence», p. 3.

y mortífera odisea» through the police cells (208), thus reversing the sexual roles and the negative outcome of the Orpheus myth. [17]

Encarna's entire adult experience has been associated with the earth. She remembers her first sexual encounter with her young husband: «cuando ella misma se siente parte de la tierra caliente como un pan bajo el sol de julio» (200). It is natural that her first-born child, a daughter, should be given the name «Florita» because she has sprung, not only from an established iconic and literary tradition represented at its best by Pedro de Espinosa's sonnet addressed to «la divina ... mi hermosa Flora», [18] but, crucially, from mother earth. Encarna's womb, then, has proved fertile, in contrast to the sterile *vientres* and *matrices* of other women in the book. The description of her sexual initiation carries some positive connotations, notwithstanding the fact that the encounter was virtually indistinguishable from rape:

> el tísico de su marido que tiene sonrisa de ratón cuando todavía es joven... abusa y la domina en una tapia de era, a la caída de la tarde..., tan lejos de toda agua, siendo ella la única cosa fresca de la tierra y lo que él necesita para calmar la sed del cuerpo. (200)

The setting of the first days of her married life «sobre los campos de trigo en la vega del Tajo» (120) recalls Molly Bloom's first love-making with Leopold «among the rhododendrons on Howth head», [19] and is an additional indication of fertility.

This mention of the river Tagus is one of many allusions to the geographical origins of Encarna's family. The narrator emphasises the apparently trivial fact that «la familia muequil» hails from Toledo by telling the reader in the opening pages that «las dos "a Toledo ortae" muchachas no rubias» gestated «en vientre toledano» (11), and, in his account of Pedro's attempts to stem the flow of blood from Florita's damaged uterus, avers that «Tratándose de hembra sana de raza toledana pareció superflua toda anestesia» (106). His words contain a substantial element of ironic black humour, yet they also articulate an incontrovertible truth, since Florita had previously enjoyed normal menstruation, being the elder of «[los] dos retoños ya menstruantes» of the family (29). Insomuch she is a healthy and positive counter-sign to Dorita's post-menopausal grandmother who bewails «la tragedia del derrumbe definitivo de mi vida de mujer» (22).

Florita is credited with definite powers of fertility. Her father entrusts her with the ritual obligation of providing Pedro with refreshing drinks of

[17] The Orphic resonances of *Tiempo de silencio* have been documented by RICARDO GULLÓN, cited in note 2 above. See also JOHN CAVIGLIA, «A Simple Question of Symmetry: Psyche as Structure in *Tiempo de silencio*», *Hispania*, LX (1977), 456.

[18] See PEDRO DE ESPINOSA, *Poesías completas*, ed. Francisco López Estrada (Madrid, 1975), p. 18.

[19] JAMES JOYCE, *Ulysses*, p. 703.

lemon and water (50), and, with her sister, she successfully incubates a strain of mice which invariably die in the laboratory of the research institute. «Pero, ¿por qué no se les mueren?» Pedro wonders: «¿Qué poder tienen las mal alimentadas muchachas toledanas para que los ratones pervivan y críen?» (12). It is a supreme and unexplained irony that the two undernourished young girls should possess «una tan genesíaca propiedad que sus efluvios emanados bastan para garantizar el reencendido del ardor genésico y la siempre continua línea de descendientes tarados» (13). Their mother contributes crucially to the working of the miracle since it is she who feeds the mice, «manten[iendo] aún firmemente en su regazo el pienso de los milagrosos ratones» (53). Martín Santos's symbolic design exhibits a remarkable consistency: just as the fertile earth assimilates seed, sustains floral growth and produces cereal crops, so Encarna, who is associated with both soil and water (the river Tagus), engenders a daughter, Florita, and distributes life-enhancing food which she holds close to her «vientre toledano».

This body of motifs is not elaborated in any mechanical way, nor does it yield up its meanings to an undiscriminating analysis. Not all the novel's Toledans are characterised by fertility. El Muecas himself originated from a «lejano pueblo toledano» (199), a detail which suggests that only female natives of Toledo are endowed with this positive quality. Yet, the example of Amador's «madre toledana» who suffers the affliction of a «seca matriz» (156) indicates that this hypothesis is only partly correct. One feels that in Martín Santos's elusive argument geographical factors alone are not sufficient to explain the physical and moral health of Encarna and Florita. An analysis of historical and social factors provides a solution to this intricate puzzle.

When Pedro visits el Muecas's house for the first time, he is welcomed with «los gestos corteses heredados desde antiguos siglos por los campesinos de la campiña toledana» (49). Notwithstanding the all-pervasive irony of the novel, it is clear that the narrative at this point projects an idealised vision of a civilised peasant class whose cultural traditions extend at least as far back as medieval times. The full historical significance of the reference to «la campiña toledana» is revealed subsequently in a related passage. As Pedro washes his face with cold water late on Saturday night, he considers the fact that Madrid in 1950 is «un pueblo que no tiene agua», and draws a contrast between the modern capital of Spain and Castile and the ancient capital and fertile kingdom of Toledo. He recalls the conquest of Alcadir's Toledo by Alfonso VI in «la lejana noche de la edad media cuando ellos con su sable levantado consiguieron dar forma a expensas de la morisma de los campos de Toledo y de las zonas bajas donde [ella, la morisma] había empezado a trabajar las huertas, a la nueva nación». Here the Alphonsine campaigns of 1081 and 1085 are viewed as a crucial stage in the reconquest and unification of modern Spain under a Catholic monarchy, but they are also presented as a concerted programme of destruction of Moorish agricultural enterprise. The fertility of the old kingdom thus gave way to the sterility of the new as the cultivated *huertas* of the Tagus valley were displaced by the «ciudad aséptica, sin huerta» of Madrid (99). Martín Santos employs this antithetical scheme to denote the submission of a racially mixed society of Jews, Moors and Mozarabic Christians to the ascendant political force of Castile, «donde el hombre se alimenta de espíritu y aire puro por los siglos de los siglos. Amén». That the metaphoric «imperio de secano» which began at the end of the eleventh century extends into the era of contemporary Spain is made clear in the concluding lines of Pedro's brooding monologue (100).

The association thus established between Toledo, its natural fertility and an antiquity pre-dating the religious and racial monolith of modern Spain provides a framework within which one can fully comprehend the significance of Encarna/Ricarda and her daughters. Encarna is identified with a pre-Alphonsine and pre-Castilian historical principle which is conceived most productively not as an essence, but as a substance. That substance is fertile, female and, in social terms, lowly; it is *incarnate* in Encarna/Ricarda whose two names, deriving respectively from Latin and Germanic sources, [20] represent a fusion of the Roman and the Visigothic strata of Spanish (and specifically, Toledan) history. It is embodied also in the flesh of her surviving daughter and, at a figurative level only, in the corpse of Florita: the exhumation of Florita's body which is then returned to her element — the earth — (195) reassures the reader that she will be substantially preserved and made fit for cyclical renewal.

The women of el Muecas's family have been forced by historical circumstance to reside in Madrid, the capital which exemplifies more than any other Spanish city the «ciudades ... tan faltas de sustancia histórica, tan traídas y llevadas por gobernantes arbitrarios, tan caprichosamente edificadas en desiertos ... que no tienen catedral» (13-15). But it is they who constitute the substance which is so conspicuously absent from the country's institutional life. They represent all that is humble and unselfish; as indicated above, they remain healthy and immune to the diseases which rack the body politic. The courage and generosity of Encarna, «la cual no había nacido para odiar» (111), is effectively an antidote to the collective hatred of a vengeful people. As a result she and her daughters may be envisaged as the beleaguered antibodies of Spanish society. Her admirable denunciation of her husband stands out as a repudiation of his authority over her, and as a self-styled liberation —or divorce— from the repressive institution of marriage which Martín Santos discredits wholesale in the pages of his novel.

[20] The Germanic origin of variants of the name «Richard» / «Ricardo» is attested by JOSEPH M. PIEL, «Antroponimia germánica», in *Enciclopedia Lingüística Hispánica*, edited by M. ALVAR, A. BADÍA, R. DE BALBÍN and L. F. LINDLEY CINTRA, 3 vols. (Madrid, 1960), I, 424-25. History manuals document the establishing of Toledo as the capital of the Visigothic Kingdom in Spain under the rule of Leovigildo (573-86 a. d.).

Our reading of *Tiempo de silencio* has focussed on several archetypal images of men and women and has identified certain figurative structures —those of family relations, fertility and disease— which form the basis of an allegorical interpretation of the novel. The character of Encarna/Ricarda plays a central role in Luis Martín Santos's critique of Spain. *Tiempo de silencio* is thus in one sense the author's idiosyncratic portrait of a lady whom he invests with particular ideological significance. The archetypal model on which her portrait is fashioned serves as a vehicle for the expression of the Spanish people's need for a redeemer. In this instance the image of the earth mother is free of any parodic or misogynistic intent which would advance the cause of male supremacy, and instead promotes the «exuberancia elemental y cíclica» (95) of *la madre España*.

The subject of portraiture is dramatised at length in a fragment which recounts Pedro and Matías's visit to the studio of two artists, one Spanish, the other German. This sequence allows the author an opportunity to combine psychoanalytical and ideological considerations with a semiological investigation into the nature of artistic representation. In the process he lays bare the foundations on which his masterpiece rests. The fragment in question contrasts pictures by the two artists and ambiguously affirms the superiority of those painted by the Spaniard whose «ideal estético» finds expression in «innumerables lienzos ... todos los cuales estaban constituidos por desnudos sonrosados de mujeres gorditas». Although his depictions of women are blatantly stereotyped: «Las sonrosadas damas sonreían estereotipadamente mediante sus rostros de pan tostado y colocaban sus miembros en las más variadas posturas siguiendo las vulgares recetas del arte combinatorio» (71-72), the deficiency implied by an apparent lack of originality is outweighed by qualities of naturalness and vitality. The narrator is impressed by the absence of «todo falso pudor» in the artist's vision and admires the results he has achieved with «elementales medios». For his part, Pedro entertains the theory that «El número de desnudos que pinta [un artista] indica el nivel alcanzado por la represión de un pueblo» (72). With this in mind, the «espacio carnal» of the Spaniard's studio comes to resemble a vast canvas or a stage on which the collective unconscious of Spanish society is projected and a symbolic release sought for the sexual and political tensions of the country.

This part of the sequence is plainly a *mise en abîme* of Martín Santos's novel which exhibits a collection of stereotyped portraits of men and women. The most *elemental* of these is the earth mother, Encarna, whose privileged position in the author's gallery is underlined by the common use of a key motif: the «rostros de pan tostado» of «las sonrosadas damas» on display adumbrate the description of her on the occasion of her sexual initiation, «cuando ella misma se siente parte de la tierra caliente como un pan bajo el sol de julio» (200). Most important of all, the symbolic resonances of her name are heightened in a rehearsed but witty exchange in Latin between Matías and Pedro, as they stare at the nudes:

—Jubilatio *in carne feminae* —inició Matías. (Our emphasis)
—Pulcritudo vastissima semper derramata —continuó Pedro. (72)

The author's quotation from an unidentified source consolidates the image of Encarna's spiritual beauty and fortifies the reader's admiration for her. It also provides renewed evidence of her and her daughter's status as martyrs. Encarna had been referred to previously as «una mártir» (33), and Florita had shown Pedro and Amador the marks of mice bites «que la calificaban como mártir de la ciencia» (53). Encarna's martyrdom takes the form of suffering the loss of a beloved daughter; because she and Florita are of the same substance, she shares in her daughter's fatal loss of blood (203). Imagery of earth, flowers and seeds nevertheless suggests a regenerative potential which helps to distinguish the women's martyrdom from that of San Lorenzo, the equivalent male type. For, whereas San Lorenzo's suffering is an image of sterility, theirs is a fertile sacrifice on behalf of the mother country.

The second part of the sequence set in the artist's studio also elucidates Martín Santos's intentions. [21] It focusses on «un cuadro realmente muy malo» painted by a ridiculed German neo-Expressionist whose canvasses are referred to disapprovingly as «los secos hijos de su espíritu» (71). Bono's painting conveys a hopeless, dehumanised view of collective suffering and is dismissed by Matías for lacking «la protoforma de la vitalidad que nace» (75). However, Pedro wonders whether Matías might not be mistaken in his evaluation of Bono's work which, it is also claimed, expresses «el pathos atormentado de un pueblo culpable y en derrota» (69). If Bono's painting is a manifestation of guilt on behalf of the traumatised German people in the aftermath of the Second World War, then it cannot be dismissed as an absolutely sterile product. Nor can we dismiss the claim that «el carácter fecaloideo del cuadro y la vermiculosidad de sus protagonistas no eran obstáculo para que fuera mirado con el fervor con que al hijo recién nacido mira una madre (no un padre)» (73). The image of a new-born child clearly invites interpretation as a positive sign of vitality, at least in the eyes of the «spiritual mother», namely, the artist himself. To match or improve on the ambiguous promise shown in Bono's painting, Martín Santos must also create a fertile work which allows for the expression of a people's tormented feelings of guilt and complicity in their own repression. *Tiempo de silencio* is that work: harsh in its vision of a people whom it depicts systematically in vegetable, animal

[21] GUSTAVO PÉREZ FIRMAT has discussed the emblematic function of Bono's painting in Martín Santos's novel, in «Repetition and Excess in *Tiempo de silencio*», 194-97. Pérez Firmat's interesting view of the novel as a «cloacal» and cancerous form implies that it, like the painting, «parecía querer expre[sar] una desesperación colectiva en la que el padecer infinitos sufrimientos se acompañara de la conciencia de la estricta justicia con que habían sido merecidos» (*Tiempo de silencio*, p. 73). The authors of this study argue against the position that *Tiempo de silencio* expresses submission to the forces of repression.

and faecal terms and whom it characterises as hateful, despairing and abject, yet, at the same time, a book rich in pathos and pregnant with a material substance personified in the redeeming figure of Encarna.

The birth of a boy child has other weighty implications since it sets in train an Oedipal conflict involving the artist himself. For, just as the son must challenge paternal authority in the Freudian scenario, so the spiritual child of the artist represents a threat to the authority of the patriarchal State. [22] A dissident artist runs the risk of incurring the wrath of the State apparatus of censorship and control, [23] but he must renounce the deterrent example of «el muchacho angustiado que piensa más en el padre ofendido que en el peso de la ley» (185) and mount a courageous assault on the institutions of repression. If he is to be an effective champion of the abused «maternal» element of society, he must also throw off «el complejo de retroceso intrafetal» (162) and adopt a mature, realistic and independent stance. Failure to do so will result in that «castración afectiva» (161) which is illustrated so chillingly in Pedro's fate at the end of *Tiempo de silencio:* «¿Pero yo, por qué no estoy más desesperado? ¿Por qué me estoy dejando capar?» (237).

Bono's painting thus raises questions about the subversive potential of certain kinds of art, of which *Tiempo de silencio* is a graphic example. That enquiry complements the discussion of the anonymous Spaniard's crude yet evocative works in such a way that the entire studio sequence operates as a gloss on Martín Santos's practice in *Tiempo de silencio.* In keeping with the novel's tendency towards symmetry and repetition, the sequence projects not one but two images of the author. The result is a multi-layered portrait of a lady, a family and a disaffected artist who intends that his readers should «volver sobre todas las leyendas negras, inclinarse sobre los prospectos de más éxito turístico de la España de pandereta, levantar la capa de barniz a cada uno de los pintores que nos han pintado y escudriñar en qué lamentable sentido tenían razón» (182).

---

[22] FREUD argues that «The beginnings of religion, ethics, society and art meet in the Oedipus complex», in *Totem and Taboo,* trans. A. A. BRILL (New York, 1946), p. 202. ERICH FROMM interprets Freud's Oedipal model as the expression of rebellion against structures of authority in patriarchal society, in *The Forgotten Language* (London, 1952), pp. 170-98.

[23] For details of Martín Santos's own experience of arrest and imprisonment on four separate occasions between 1957 and 1962, see ESPERANZA G. SALUDES, *La narrativa de Luis Martín Santos a la luz de la psicología* (Miami, 1981), pp. 177-78. JANET WINECOFF DÍAZ mentions the effects of censorship on *Tiempo de silencio* in «Luis Martín Santos and the Contemporary Spanish Novel», *Hispania,* LI (1968), 234.

3

SI TE DICEN QUE CAÍ: A FAMILY AFFAIR

Si te dicen que caí, the fifth and most controversial novel by Juan Marsé, was doubly distinguished on the occasion of its publication in Mexico in 1973 by the award of the first Premio Internacional de Novela México and the simultaneous decision of the Franco administration to prohibit its widespread distribution in the author's native country. Only after three years and in the wake of the Generalísimo's death would Seix Barral launch a Spanish follow-up to the Mexican first edition which had already made a forceful impact in enlightened reading circles. By the early 1980s a consolidated critical bibliography had established guide lines for a proper appreciation of the book's infinitely complex narrative and thematic mechanisms.

The most noteworthy feature of *Si te dicen que caí* is the intricacy of its discursive structure, a feature studied in some depth by Linda Gould Levine and Diane Garvey. The discovery of traces of irreducible and wilful confusion in the narrative has not hindered the development of a general consensus about its over-all meaning. Ms. Levine's view that *Si te dicen que caí* renders faithfully «las humillaciones, torturas y soledad de los años cuarenta en España»[1] is echoed in Geneviève Champeau's reading of the novel as a forceful evocation of «la degradation avec toutes ses variantes (prostitution, perversion, humiliation, corruption)»;[2] Juan Marsé confirms that these were the defining characteristics of a period of «represión social, política, cultural, de todo tipo ...».[3] Critics also agree that the intended aim of Marsé's chronicle of «tantos años de paz y penicilina»[4] is to articulate, and thus preserve, the collective memory of an urban community representative of the country as a whole, in the confidence that «el poder polí-

---

[1] LINDA GOULD LEVINE, «*Si te dicen que caí:* un calidoscopio verbal», *Journal of Spanish Studies: Twentieth Century,* VII (1979), 309-27 (p. 314).

[2] GENEVIÈVE CHAMPEAU, «A propos de *Si te dicen que caí*», *Bulletin Hispanique,* LXXXV, nos. 3-4 (1983), 359-78 (p. 374).

[3] See the author's declarations reproduced by SHIRLEY MANGINI GONZÁLEZ, «El punto de vista dual en tres novelistas españoles», *Insula,* 396-97 (Nov.-Dec. 1979), p. 7.

[4] JUAN MARSÉ, *Si te dicen que caí,* first edition (Barcelona, 1979), p. 288. Page references to this edition will be included in the text.

tico tendrá que rendir cuentas a esta memoria colectiva que, quiérase o no, acabará por imponerse».[5]

Where opinion tends to fragment is in assessing the relative importance and integrity of the novel's many story lines. Cast in the mould of popular adventure stories («aventis»), the narrative of *Si te dicen que caí* spans a period of thirty years up to the early nineteen seventies and plots the changes which occur during that time in the attitudes and fortunes of at least six major characters: Daniel Javaloyes (known in his youth as Java), his elder brother Marcos, Ñito (who as a boy was called Sarnita), Aurora Nin (alias Ramona), Carmen (also known as Menchu), and Conrado Galán, as well as a host of secondary figures. Carmen's story, which follows the spectacular progress of a «fulana de lujo» in the «new» Spain of General Franco and culminates with an account of her violent death on a cold January night in 1949, is typical of a general pattern: while it coincides disconcertingly at several points with the story of Ramona, it nevertheless possesses sufficient clarity of outline to be considered a self-contained unit. At the same time, Carmen's experience describes a process of corruption and decline which informs all of the stories in the book and may as a result be read as a synecdoche, a part which is representative of a complex but harmonious whole.

This perception of unity is at variance with the views of some like Diane Garvey who maintain that «In *Si te dicen que caí*, there is no one "story", or "plot", no rounded characters or consistent symbolism».[6] In our view this opinion requires reappraisal. A detailed re-examination of the relationship between character and narrative structure in *Si te dicen que caí* promises to enhance our appreciation of the integrity of this elusive text. Discussion of Marsé's use of visual material will, it is hoped, both provide valuable supporting evidence of coherence and illuminate the historical and ideological content of his novel.

In their analyses of the narrative design of *Si te dicen que caí* several commentators grant pride of place in it to Ramona, «la puta roja» (73). Ms. Levine's assertion that Ramona is «la fuerza principal detrás de la narración»[7] has the persuasive force of consensus and is borne out, though not unreservedly, by a declaration made by the author himself:

> La caza y la captura de una meuca en la posguerra era precisamente el tema inicial de mi *aventi*. Pero en seguida, una célula en algún rincón de la memoria, anestesiada por la represión franquista, empezó a despertar lenta- mente y me entregó el contexto histórico, la crónica de una década atroz.[8]

[5] See JUAN MARSÉ, *Confidencias de un chorizo* (Barcelona, 1977), p. 174.
[6] DIANE GARVEY, «Juan Marsé's *Si te dicen que caí*: the Self-reflexive Text and the Question of Referentiality», *MLN*, vol. 95 (1980), 376-87 (p. 386).
[7] LINDA GOULD LEVINE, «*Si te dicen que caí*: un calidoscopio verbal», p. 313.
[8] JUAN MARSÉ, *Confidencias de un chorizo*, p. 172.

It is important to note that while Marsé acknowledges the crucial role of a historical figure who was to be the model for his characterisation of Ramona, he nevertheless insists on the primacy of an overall design to which individual characters would be subordinated. This far from exceptional observation acquires unexpected significance in the light of Gregorio Morán's conclusion that a completely different character performs the role of protagonist in the novel. Morán singles out for attention the figure of Java the rag-and-bone boy, in whom he perceives an example of the type of the *trepador,* or social climber, found throughout Marsé's work. [9] There is certainly a strong case for highlighting the biography of this character who progresses literally from rags to riches before meeting his death in a motor accident. Laid out on a mortuary slab, «Este trapero que al cabo de treinta años alcanzaba su corrupción final enmascarado de dignidad y dinero» (13) is a graphic emblem of the social decay which is portrayed systematically at every level of the book. Sarnita reveals the unsavoury truths which are concealed behind the façade of Daniel's material success when he describes him as «un mariquita de medio pelo» who «nunca se lanzó a fondo, nunca consintió por placer o debilidad sino por abrirse camino» (349). Yet, for all its singularity and wealth of meaning, Java's story cannot be considered in isolation from other biographies in the book; the text itself suggests as much and goes some way towards correcting a discrete view of the characters. When Sarnita tells Justiniano, the one-eyed Falangist and district boss, his version of «[la] historia del escondido y la raspa perseguida» (267), he recognises that Ramona's story is inseparable from that of the outlawed terrorist, Marcos Javaloyes, who lives in hiding behind a false wall at the back of the family *trapería* from which he emerges only at night to «estirar las piernas por el barrio» (95) and to meet his fellow *maquis* at the Alaska Bar. Marcos and Ramona are indeed bound to each other by «un amor imposible» (345) and die together hand in hand, killed by an exploding shell as they run across some open ground escaping from the vengeful Justiniano and his henchmen.

However, even Sarnita's «versión del asunto» of *Si te dicen que caí* is deficient, because it fails to account for Java's crucial involvement in the deaths of Marcos and Ramona whom he betrays in exchange for help in furthering his career. In the course of a conversation with Justiniano Java feigns contempt for the class of «soplones de la bofia capaces de vender a su propia madre» (296) but does not hesitate to reveal Ramona's hiding place, thereby setting in motion a sequence of events culminating in a trap which he springs on his own brother. That outcome exposes the cringing hypocrisy of his earlier protestations:

[9] GREGORIO MORÁN, «*Si te dicen que caí*», *Cuadernos Para el Diálogo,* 178 (25 September 1976), p. 50.

¿Qué se puede decir de una aventi de Sarnita que empieza diciendo qué se puede decir de una puta roja que empieza diciendo qué decir del hombre que amo y vive oculto varios metros bajo tierra con su mecedora y sus crucigramas y que dice no volveré a ver el sol, Aurora, mi hermano nos traicionará? (292)

and places him at the exact centre of a web of relationships and incidents which make up «la intríngulis» of *Si te dicen que caí* (40). Java's relationship with Marcos and Ramona constitutes a by no means original love triangle which unites both the young and the adult groups of protagonists. In a second triangle he competes with Conrado for the affections of la Fueguiña, but his relationship with Marcos and Ramona is of greater thematic importance because it provides for the betrayal of a brother in the chillingly appropriate context of the aftermath of a war which, by definition, was fratricidal.[10] In our view this is the crux of the book: *Si te dicen que caí* is a topical family drama which reworks the theme of fratricide expressed memorably in «La tierra de Alvargonzález» by Antonio Machado and *Abel Sánchez* by Miguel de Unamuno, and present in an attenuated form both in *Nada* by Carmen Laforet and, more obliquely, Saura's *La caza*.

Juan Marsé intensifies the drama of the Javaloyes family by endowing the two brothers with a certain physical resemblance. When Java and Ramona had been summoned to the *comisaría de la Travesera* to answer questions concerning Marcos's whereabouts, she had told the young *trapero*: «Te pareces a alguien que un día amé mucho» (296). Java mentions this detail twice when he talks subsequently to Justiniano, and is clearly aware of its implications. In his determination to dissociate himself from Marcos he insists that «no nos parecemos en nada» (299), but the narrative confirms Ramona's impression: Java's swarthy complexion and «frente llena de rizos» (22) duplicate two of the recorded traits of Marcos's physiognomy, ie., his brown skin and curly hair.

The duplication of characters is a recognised hallmark of Marsé's technique in this and other novels, a practice generally understood in relation to a concern with personal identity. In this case, the question of doubles may be considered just as fruitfully in relation to the figurative structure of the family. Critical writing on Marsé attaches surprisingly little importance to the fact that the motor accident which ends Daniel Javaloyes's sterile life also kills his wife and their two children; yet this anecdotal detail possesses immense significance, for Java and Pilar's children are identical twins whose character is summed up by a relative who goes to the hospital to collect their belongings:

[10] PAUL ILIE touches on the theme of fratricide in Marsé's novel in a stimulating study concerned primarily with the marginalisation of the citizens of Barcelona in the early post-war years. See his *Literature and Inner Exile. Authoritarian Spain, 1939-1975* (Baltimore & London, 1980), pp. 93-113 (103).

Qué extraños eran, dijo, nunca les entendí, tan formalitos por separado, tan normales y hasta anodinos, y juntos qué malos, qué embusteros y vengativos. (192)

Born of a treacherous father, the twins embody a heritage of deceit and vengefulness which Marsé suggests is inherent in the family of Spain. It is tempting to see behind their fortuitous death the hand of the author who pretends to excise those destructive traits from the Spanish national character by means of a ruthless fictional murder. Such a hypothesis, though, is negated by the recurrent image of the scorpion, «un bicho que trae mala suerte y representa el odio entre hermanos, la capacidad de autodestrucción que hay en el hombre» (129). Appearing in the form of a medallion on a gold bracelet that belongs to Menchu, the scorpion does indeed bring bad luck to all who touch it and is at once an emblem, as it had been in Buñuel's early masterpiece, *L'Age d'Or,* of the vicious disunity of the nation, and a symbol of the relationship between Daniel and Marcos Javaloyes. The most awesome of its negative attributes is its power to survive in the most inhospitable of environments: in the devastated setting of post-war Barcelona *un muchacho del Carmelo* tells an oracular *aventi* about «venenosos escorpiones que sobre-vivirán a estas ruinas» (171) and thus conveys a profoundly pessimistic inter-pretation of the character and prospects of the Spanish people.

An essential aspect of Marsé's critique of Spain is a historical perspective which embraces and illuminates the prolonged «noche negra» of Francoism. That perspective acquires added breadth through repeated references which are made to «un cuadro famoso» (200) depicting an execution scence of «un borroso amanecer en la playa y unos hombres antiguos y lívidos maniatados junto a un fraile capuchino» (21). We can identify the picture as *El fusila-miento del general Torrijos y sus compañeros* by Antonio Gisbert (1835-1902), housed in the Casón del Buen Retiro in Madrid (see Plate 1). Torrijos was executed on the beach at Málaga in December 1831 for conspiring against the monarchy of Ferdinand VII and was proclaimed a martyr by fellow Liberals like Espronceda who commemorated him in a famous poem entitled «A la muerte de Torrijos». Especially relevant here is the fact that the young officer, then in exile, was lured into a trap by General Vicente González Moreno, the Military Governor of Málaga, who encouraged him to spearhead an uprising against the Crown under assurances that there would be massive support waiting for him on the Andalusian coast. When Torrijos landed with his companions at Fuengirola he was promptly captured and condemned to death, the victim of an insidious manoeuvre master-mind-ed by a fellow officer whose act of treachery may be seen both as the reenactment of an archetype and as a historical precedent for Java's fiction-al betrayal of Marcos in *Si te dicen que caí*.

Gisbert's painting of Torrijos's execution is recalled up to a dozen times in the course of the novel. It figures prominently in the opening chapter where we learn that a reproduction of it appears in the pattern of a carpet found in the crippled Falangist, Conrado Galán's bedroom. The narrative recounts Java's first visit to Conrado's apartment, tracing his steps along «un oscuro corredor en cuyas paredes desfilan profundos ejércitos en campaña, sangrientas cargas de caballería con alazanes encabritados entre nubes de polvo, y armaduras fantasmales» and describing his cautious entry into the bedroom. As the door shuts behind him «como una trampa» (20-21) he finds himself ensnared in the company of a girl he has never previously met but with whom he will perform violent and degrading sexual acts at Conrado's command. At an early stage of their mechanical proceedings Ramona puts herself at Java's mercy, crouching over the carpet and

> arrastrándose mientras la azota con el cordón, [Ramona] volvería a inmovilizarse, a ovillarse sobre los fusilados con la cabeza entre los brazos. Sudando Java tira el cordón y ella clava las rodillas en la arena manchada de sangre entre la cabeza destrozada y el sombrero de copa caído. (29)

The deliberate confusion of grammatical values and of different orders of reality ensures the impact of a scene which in essence superimposes one image of victimization (Java abusing Ramona) on another (the firing squad executing one of Torrijos's men).

The roles of victim and victimizer illustrated in this sequence are reversed in a subsequent encounter between Java and the homosexual Ado who waits for him in Conrado's bed like a «pantera al acecho», having undressed and left his shoes on the carpet «sobre la cabeza de Torrijos». Java facilitates Ado by lying with «la cabeza colgando fuera de la cama, mordiéndose el labio a un palmo de la alfombra», and sees in the reproduction of Gisbert's painting an unflattering representation of himself as «una carne yerta que mucho antes de sonar la descarga ya había dejado de recibir el flujo de la sangre». The crude sexual imagery of «la descarga» does little to embellish the scene, but the resemblance between Ado and Java reverberates at the deepest level of the novel's thematic structure. Gazing at Ado, Java realises that «Era su vivo retrato: la misma piel morena y sedosa, el mismo pelo negro ensortijado y los mismos ojos, estirados hacia las sienes» (285). Through this duplication Marsé locates Java and Ado's sexual intercourse within a paradigm of acts of aggression which, because they are directed against one's *alter ego* —a twin brother of look-alike, a fellow countryman or, in the case of Torrijos and González Moreno, a fellow officer— are a threat to the integrity of the self.

The antagonism between rival groups of Spaniards in the critical period of the 1930s and 40s is the clearest example of that model of behaviour. Using Gisbert's painting as a point of reference, Marsé evokes the executions carried out on the beaches of Catalonia by Nationalist firing squads after the official end of the Civil War. With his usual mastery of double-talk, Sarnita mentions reports of «denuncias y revanchas y hasta fusilamientos cada nuevo amanecer en la playa» only to dismiss them as «patrañas inventadas por los rojos» (261). But the grisly fate of an inmate of Barcelona's Modelo prison gives the lie to his claim and makes it clear that such purges did take place «en la rompiente del campo de la Bota» and at other sites on the coast around Barcelona (183). In effect, the motif of the beach at daybreak establishes an unmistakable association between vanquished Republicans and Torrijos's men and, by extension, equates the intransigence of Franco's Nationalists with the repressive zeal of Fernandine Absolutists. By drawing on this and other details of Gisbert's painting, Marsé achieves a literary expression of the conventional historical view that the origins of political conflict in twentieth-century Spain lie in the period when parliamentary democracy first struggled to reform the *ancien régime* and met with a fiercely polarised reaction.

The painting of Torrijos's execution is the first of many visual references incorporated into the narrative of *Si te dicen que caí*. Marsé also cites a dozen or so film titles, all of which are fittingly associated with the classical period of English and American cinema of the 30s and 40s. Titles such as «Las Aventuras de Marco Polo» (234) and «Los Tambores de Fu Man Chu» (259) are an indication of the young protagonists' taste in films, which Marsé records with psychological as well as historical accuracy. The films which he mentions also fulfil specific roles within the narrative and thematic structure of his novel. Two of those cited mirror the characters' circumstances, but at a rather trivial level. Intent on flattering Justiniano whom he praises as «un héroe que dio un ojo por la causa», Sarnita compares him somewhat predictably with «el almirante Nelson en Lady Hamilton» (257), an English film directed by Alexander Korda in 1941. Elsewhere, in one of their make-believe interrogations, the delinquent boys threaten la Fueguiña («canta si no quieres ser la Mujer Marcada», p. 144) with a form of punishment reminiscent of the fate of Bette Davis in Lloyd Bacon's film of 1937. The facial burns which la Fueguiña suffers in her rescue of Conrado towards the end of the novel evoke just as precisely the disfigurement of Joan Crawford in *A Woman's Face* (directed by George Cukor in 1941). Other films provide more substantial points of contact with the story of *Si te dicen que caí*. In *The Prisoner of Zenda* (directed by John Cromwell in 1937 and mentioned on p. 173 of Marsé's novel), a treacherous count plots to remove his brother, Rudolf, from the throne of Ruritania and is thwarted by the King's double, an English cousin called Rudolf Rassendyll who saves the nation and charms the King's bride-to-be. Java's underhand actions and usurping of his brother's girl friend may be seen as a debased version of the dashing Rassendyll's heroics. An identical combination of the theme of treachery, the topos of the double and a triangular relationship between one woman and two men who look alike is also found in *Arsène Lupin* which Jack Conway directed in 1932 after the famous stories and play of the same title by Maurice Leblanc. This popular film of intrigue and deceit starred the brothers John and Lionel Barrymore in a fast-moving story which includes a jewel robbery, a scene of entrapment, and the assumption of a false identity by one male character (Lupin) who succeeds another (the Duc de Charmerace) as a rich girl's fiancé; Lupin's resemblance to the Duke is such that he exclaims in the original script «On aurait dit deux frères jumeaux». [11] Sarnita's comment that a coincidence such as this «sólo pasa en el cine y aun así es mentira, son dobles» (259) does nothing to diminish the importance of a motif which is central to the novel and a key element in its interaction with the world of the screen.

The degree of prominence which Gisbert's painting, John Cromwell's film and Jack Conway's version of *Arsène Lupin* enjoy in the structure of *Si te dicen que caí* is a measure of Marsé's fascination with, and indebtedness to, the visual world; indeed, he is on record as saying that «Yo normalmente escribo estimulado por imágenes, no por ideas». [12] That visual bias is noticeable from the first lines of his novel which freeze the moment at which Nito «levanta el borde de la sábana que cubría al ahogado» and stares into Daniel's «ojos abiertos» (13). The narrative will describe other moments of visual discovery and dramatise repeatedly the act of peering through «el turbio cristal» (254) which represents the obscure forms of vision prevalent in post-war Spanish society. Marcos's «gafas negras de ciego que camuflaban sus famosos ojos azules» (293) exemplify the blinkered vision of the *maquis* (95), and Java's «ojos enfermos de legañas, pelones y rojos» (238) betoken an inner sickness whose symptoms are also visible in Conrado's eyes (353). Justiniano is a suggestive figure in this regard: «El único ojo del delegado, negro, insistente» (132) recalls both the monstrosity of the mythical Cyclops and the «dark eyes» of BIG BROTHER which «looked deep into Winston's own» in an early sequence of George Orwell's *Nineteen Eighty-Four*. [13] As the State's delegate and watchdog, Justiniano wields frightening powers of control and arrest and protects its interests by fostering an «horrible atmósfera de sospechas y espionitis» (68). The characters of *Si te dicen que caí* spy on one another indiscriminately in the pursuit of political and sexual goals which are sick and perverted. Conrado admits to Ramona, after she catches him spying on her innocent love-making with Pedro, that his voyeurism «era como una enfermedad» (246). As Geneviève Champeau has observed, [14] Conrado is in fact an outrageous caricature of General Franco: described as a «soldadito de plomo» who suffers from Parkinson's disease (198 & 331), he, like the motionless protagonist of Saura's *El jardín de las delicias* (1970), represents the paralysis of post-war

[11] FRANCIS DE CROISSET & MAURICE LEBLANC, «Arsène Lupin», in *L'Illustration Théâtrale*, 115 (27 March 1909), p. 35.
[12] See JACK SINNIGEN, «Entrevista con Juan Marsé», in *Narrativa e ideología* (Madrid, 1982), pp. 111-22 (p. 117).
[13] GEORGE ORWELL, *Nineteen Eighty-Four* (Harmondsworth, 1977), p. 6.
[14] GENEVIÈVE CHAMPEAU, «À propos de *Si te dicen que caí*», pp. 365-66.

politics, the inner putrefaction and perversion of authority. In addition, Conrado's pathological condition provides a yard-stick for measuring the sickness of an entire society, since his voyeuristic compulsion is typical of the sexual behaviour of countless others including Ñito and Mianet, who derive excitement from spying on unsuspecting young women, and Paulina, la Fueguiña and Ramona who all find pleasure in contemplating scenes of violence and degradation. A phrase which Java uses to describe his brother's circumstances is readily applicable to the vast majority of characters in Marsé's novel: «la vida vista por un agujero» (294) connotes both the narrowness of their perspective on life and the filtering of sense impressions through the distorting lens of sexuality.

The third eye, or «ojete» (in Spanish, «anus»), [15] through which these *mirones* perceive reality also connotes the aperture of a camera or film projector. The presence, in the narrative of *Si te dicen que caí,* of a set of images of shadows (144), a silhouette (344) and «una lluvia de sangre» which «una lámpara de flecos rojos» projects onto a wall (97) reinforces that analogy and strengthens the connexion between Marsé's book and the world of the screen. We have already noted how cinematic allusions illuminate configurations of character in the novel and underline its principal thematic designs; they also bring sharply into focus crucial questions about realism and genre, as the example of *Arsène Lupin* again demonstrates.

The film of *Arsène Lupin* is featured at a climactic moment of the narrative when Java discovers Ramona in the darkness of the Roxy cinema and propositions her to the accompaniment of scenes from Jack Conway's film. At the beginning of the episode the fictitious romance between a debonair gentleman and «una dama de luminosos hombros desnudos» reflects ironically on the grimy rag-and-bone boy's affair with *la puta roja* and consigns it to a wholly inferior realm of experience. But it is not long before the sophisticated world of art becomes contaminated by the contents of Ramona's mind which she projects onto the screen:

> En la pantalla unos chillidos de mujer, los faros de un automóvil en la noche, parado en la carretera, y un hombre asustado debatiéndose entre sus dos verdugos; un tercero sacando la pistola y la mujer chillando no le matéis, ése no es Arsenio Lupin, no le matéis. (176)

The death of an innocent man is the stuff of «un mal sueño» (174) which has haunted Ramona ever since the time when, at the beginning of the Civil War, she denounced the young Conrado to her uncle, the Anarchist Artemio Nin, and then failed to take any action as the murder squad under his command detained and shot not him, but his father. In the cinema Java misin-

---

[15] JUAN GOYTISOLO discusses the subversive force of the image of the «ojo del culo», in «Quevedo: la obsesión excremental», in *Disidencias* (Barcelona, 1977), pp. 117-35.

terprets the cause of her agitation and tries to comfort her by saying that what she has seen «no es más que una peli» (176). However, Martín asserts elsewhere that «Hay pelis que son verdad» (103), thereby confirming the complex interrelationship between art and reality in Marsé's novel.

The climactic episode of Ramona, Java and his celluloid double, Arsène Lupin, brings together themes of darkness, violence and degraded sexuality which are typical of the world of the cinema depicted in *Si te dicen que caí*. For example, the assassination of a policeman by some *maquis* takes place in *El Cine Roxy*, the victim being gunned down as he goes to investigate some suspicious goings-on in the stalls (69). Cinemas are also the setting of ritual obedience «cuando tocan el himno» (121) and, at the same time, the haunt of *pajilleras* and other individuals who, like John Schlesinger's Midnight Cowboy, are the confused protagonists of squalid sexual encounters. Through these connotations Marsé conjures up a menacing and unnatural realm of darkness and half-light which acts as a powerful metaphor for the violent repression and degradation of Spanish society in the post-war years.

The generic properties of his novel reinforce that critical intent. *Si te dicen que caí* incorporates aspects of several film and literary genres, most notably crime detection and gangsterism, the spy thriller, horror, and erotic subject matter, all of which dramatise the conflict between the forces of anarchy and principles of social order. Many of the characters in the novel «pare[cían] jugar a detectives» (73) in the manner of Sherlock Holmes (333) or Ironside (102). In their efforts to determine «cuándo y cómo empezó la persecución de la puta roja, quién lo sabe, quién tuvo la culpa» (73), Sarnita and Java engage in «pesquisas» and follow up clues —«pistas» (165)— which belong to the same category as «ces indices ... ces pistes qui se croisent» in Leblanc's masterpiece of crime detection.[16] The gangster movie leaves a legacy of debts, including the use of aliases and disguises and the reliance on character types like the gangster's Moll, here remoulded in the composite figure of Ramona-Menchu who is destined to be Marcos's «espía y su aventurera, su rubia platino, su mujer fatal» (267), and the *pistolero* «sobre cuya frente resbala un sombrero de ala torcida» (14) and who excels in the use of a patently phallic Colt 42 in the robbery at the Ritz Hotel.[17]

The spy thriller inspires both Java «cuando cuenta una de espías» (83) and Sarnita who makes up several tall versions of the «historia del escondido y la raspa perseguida» and remarks to Justiniano que «Todo esto parece un complot remoto» (269). Justiniano is the central figure of horror in *Si te dicen que caí* where he is presented as a bloodthirsty vampire. When Luisito visits the Consulate of Siam in San Gervasio and discovers that the

---

[16] FRANCIS DE CROISSET and MAURICE LEBLANC, «Arsène Lupin», p. 24.
[17] For a perceptive study of Marsé's use elsewhere of motifs from the gangster film, see JOHN P. DEVLIN, «Killing the Hero: Image and Meaning in Juan Marsé's *Un día volveré*», in *Essays in Honour of Robert Brian Tate from his Colleagues and Pupils*, ed. R. A. CARDWELL (Nottingham, 1984), pp. 29-37.

building houses a *cheka* where political prisoners are interrogated and tortured, his imagination, which is full of Mianet's tales about «niños que raptaban para chuparles la sangre» (313), transforms Justiniano and his seven assistants into «vampiros disfrazados de falangistas y de polis, tísicos perdidos, chupadores de sangre rematados» (317). It is wholly in keeping with this atmosphere of irrationality that Luisito's own death from tuberculosis should be seen as the work of Justiniano's monsters who, according to Sarnita,

> lo vaciaron, chavales, y desde entonces ya no hizo nada bueno, se ha muerto por falta de sangre, tenía que acabar así, el pobre, todos acabaremos así. (320)

Sarnita's premonition of a horrific fate which awaits the members of his generation coincides with the vampire imagery of Saura's *Cría cuervos* and bears witness to the expressive potential of this classic horror motif in the imaginative reconstruction of life under a dictatorship.

The influence of the type of erotic film generally associated with directors like Joseph Lewis and Luis Buñuel is clearly visible in this novel by Juan Marsé who admits that «A mí, el erotismo en la novela siempre me ha interesado mucho». [18] The following profile of Lewis provides a revealing comparison with Marsé's own practice:

> Most expert at illuminating the shady underside of the sexual impulse. Lewis peopled his films with fetishists and haunted men. [19]

These words capture the essence of Marsé's fictional world and evoke precisely the sickness and torment of Conrado who, as a young man, would enter the bedroom immediately after Ramona and Pedro had left and prolong the excitement caused by the sight of their love-making by

> rastreando en la cama, husmeando las sábanas, las toallas, la almohada, olfateando como un perrito el olor de sus cabellos, de su piel, midiendo con la imaginación el hueco de sus cuerpos en el colchón, calibrando su peso, oyendo sus gemidos. (144)

After he is wounded in the war and confined to a wheel-chair Conrado develops more sinister voyeuristic tendencies including acts of flagellation and bondage and various perversions performed by members of either sex.

---

[18] See JACK SINNIGEN, «Entrevista con Juan Marsé», p. 121.
[19] See JOHN BAXTER, *The Gangster Film* (New York, 1970), p. 74. A film directed by LEWIS, *Boys of the City* (1940), is of particular interest because it closely resembles *Si te dicen que caí* in subject matter and atmosphere. The title «La ciudad de los muchachos» which appears on page 193 of the novel may be a reference to Lewis's film or, alternatively, to NORMAN TAUROG's famous 1938 film, *Boys' Town,* starring Spencer Tracy and Mickey Rooney.

The portrayal of sexual relations in *Si te dicen que caí* is totally in line with Sarnita's understanding that

> Toda historia de amor, chaval, por romántica que te la quieran endilgar, no es más que un camelo para camuflar con bonitas frases algunas marranaditas tipo te besaré el coño hasta morir, vida mía, o métemela dentro hasta tocarme el corazón, niño, hasta el fin del mundo: cosas que no pueden ser, hombre. (255)

Java and Ramona's encounter in Conrado's apartment is a striking illustration of the degradation of human values implied in Sarnita's words. Their mechanical motions of desire reach such extremes of physical intensity that Ramona loses her hold on the last vestige of morality and «sólo dice en voz muy baja mátame, dos veces al final, mátame»; the implied author's comment that Java «nunca supo si fue queriendo o sin querer» (30) opens up a vista onto the most sombre realms of sexuality.

To read the harrowing episode of their prostitution is to assume inescapably the role of spectator at a peep show. Marsé's novel constructs for the reader a sordid and fetishistic perspective on human relations which makes no allowances for prudery or romantic idealism. Female characters are presented in a particularly ignoble light, being invariably the objects of a sexist gaze which fetishises knees («rodillas de seda», 273) and thighs («muslos de locura», 216). Carmen is described obsessively in those terms: when she starts work as a baroness's maid (152), when she auditions for a job as a chorus girl (215), when she is established as a «fulana de lujo» in Room 333 at the Hotel Ritz (95), and when her battered corpse is disinterred and laid out «boca arriba y con los ojos abiertos llenos de tierra ..., la cicatriz abierta en el cuello y la rodilla un poco alzada, la cara interna del muslo aún con un temblor, una carne más pálida que el resto, casi luminosa» (343). By introducing a note of eroticism into this morbid scene (see, too, the description of Luisito's mother who inadvertently displays «el trocito de muslo blanco como la nieve» to the mourners who file past his corpse, p. 312), Marsé flies in the face of decorum and reminds us, first, of Freud's thoughts on the connection between the death instinct and the libido, and, second, of Buñuel's characteristic obsession with these themes, as we later argue, in *Viridiana*.

Morbid and sordid sex, gangster violence, horror and intrigue are the subject matter of artistic genres which in their crudest manifestations seek only to simulate excitement and dispense cheap thrills. Marsé's narrators pursue those crude ideals without restraint through the fabrication of oral *aventis* which are designed to excite and intrigue. But, in their most sophisticated forms those genres mediate searching criticism of deficiencies in social and political organization. Such is the case of the classical gangster films of the 1940s, a genre constantly striving to hold up «a mirror to the subterranean discontent with the American social structure».[20] The conventions of the genres incorporated into the narrative of *Si te dicen que caí* serve the same ideological function and allow Marsé to expose the monstrous underside of Spanish society in the same period.

The risks involved in such an ambitious project are considerable: Marsé's own *aventi* might degenerate into a vulgar celebration of the degradation of fellow Spaniards both male and female; his appeal to the reader's curiosity and to the voyeuristic instinct which Freud regarded as a natural part of our psychological make-up, but one which is susceptible to perversion,[21] could also pander to the tastes of the ideologically unregenerate. In our opinion, those dangers are effectively neutralised by the dialectical processes which operate in his narrative. For, while *Si te dicen que caí* reproduces the most distorted and sordid perspectives of human behaviour, it also calls attention to the artifice at the root of its own construction, openly acknowledging its reliance on the conventions and clichés of genres which no experienced reader would take to be anything but codified representations of reality. The novel's self-conscious concern with the principle and mechanisms of representation[22] is a constant reminder that all versions of reality are constructed by the forces of artistic convention and the requirements of ideology. In writing his highly partial «crónica de una década atroz» Marsé assumes the responsibility of countering official interpretations of the realities of Spanish society in the post-war period with a no less distorted «versión del asunto» which, when placed alongside the «patrañas» of State propaganda, may reveal «una tercera dimensión de la realidad al margen de la verdad y la mentira». Dialectical procedures are therefore a fundamental part of the author's strategy and the key to the success of a project whose goal is «la recuperación de la historia».[23]

* * *

The results of our analysis endorse the standard appraisal of Juan Marsé as a leading exponent of the dialectical mode of realism initiated by Caballero Bonald and Martín Santos in the early 60s. The younger author in fact recapitulates and elaborates on several features of his predecessors' work. His depiction of the «fachadas leprosas» of buildings in a derelict

[20] See RICHARD GRIFFITH, «Cycles and Genres», in *Movies and Methods* (Berkeley, Los Angeles & London, 1976), pp. 111-18 (p. 116).

[21] FREUD discusses the perversion of the normal pleasure in looking in «The Sexual Aberrations», in *On Sexuality. Three Essays on the Theory of Sexuality and Other Works,* trans. JAMES STRACHEY and ed. ANGELA RICHARDS (Harmondsworth, 1984), pp. 69-70.

[22] PERE GIMFERRER discusses this aspect of the text in «La última novela de Juan Marsé», *Destino,* 8 March 1974, p. 29.

[23] See JACK SINNIGEN, «Entrevista con Juan Marsé», p. 118. Marsé's dialectical practice is studied by WILLIAM M. SHERZER, *Juan Marsé: entre la ironía y la dialéctica* (Madrid, 1982).

quarter of Barcelona (15) whose inhabitants are downgraded to the level of animal life mirrors Martín Santos's portrayal of the cancerous setting and subhuman living conditions in parts of post-war Madrid. His vision of the corrupt state of national institutions is also reminiscent of that of Martín Santos and is founded on an identical postulate of a deep-seated relation between sexual perversion and the abuse of power. The grotesque figure of Conrado, the transvestite policeman «vestido de andaluza» (235), the homosexual bishop whose «amor paternal es igual para todos [y] no tiene preferencias» (107), and the many father figures who abuse their authority and neglect their obligations in an orphaned society: all of these characters stand in a direct line of descent from the phallocentric ogres of *Tiempo de silencio*.

Elements of Caballero Bonald's pathological vision also appear in *Si te dicen que caí*. Ramona's «pesadillas de sangre que no la dejaban dormir» (135) recall Joaquín's psychological trauma and have similar origins in war-time experience; the horrific details of Joaquín's nightmare are also brought gruesomely to life in Marsé's tableau of the *cheka* in San Gervasio (314-20). The author's description of *Si te dicen que caí* as «un vómito de un niño-adulto que intenta ... liberarse del miedo y del asco, de la suciedad, suciedad física y espiritual, moral de unos determinados años», [24] elaborates on a central motif of *Dos días de setiembre* concerning the characters' need there to «vomitar de una vez el asqueroso cieno de la memoria» (p. 125).

These coincidences of language, attitude and sensibility are evidence of a substantial affinity between the three authors and their works which project complementary images of life under the Franco dictatorship. For the specific purpose of this study we highlight a final aspect of the interrelationship between Juan Marsé, José Manuel Caballero Bonald and Luis Martín Santos, which is their predilection for the media of painting and film, and their skill in integrating visual material into the verbal fabric of their novels. In *Si te dicen que caí*, a book which is at once the fictional equivalent of an echo chamber and a hall of mirrors —a «cárcel de espejos repetidos» (222)— Marsé takes to its furthest extreme the visual orientation which also distinguishes *Dos días de setiembre* and *Tiempo de silencio*, and illustrates most forcefully the claim, made by one of Juan Goytisolo's disenchanted narrators, that

> no es oficio ni profesión sino tormento y castigo vivir, ver, anotar, retratar cuanto sucede en tu patria. [25]

---

[24] This and other remarks by the author are reproduced in «La última novela secuestrada», *El Noticiero Universal* (Barcelona), 2 November 1976, p. 15.
[25] JUAN GOYTISOLO, *Señas de identidad* (Barcelona, 1984), p. 110.

4

VIRIDIANA AND THE DEATH INSTINCT

When Salvador Dalí, Buñuel's collaborator on *Un chien andalou* (1929) and *L'Age d'Or* (1930) first saw *Tristana* (1970), he remarked, «Se ve que a Buñuel le gusta mucho España».[1] Dalí's views are equally applicable to *Viridiana* (1961) where, just as much as in films made in Mexico or France, Buñuel's peninsular loyalties shine through the international, Latin American or Gallic persona. He himself explained his return to Spain for the filming of *Viridiana* like this: «I went back to Spain from Mexico because that is my country and I could work there with total freedom. I did work there on *Viridiana* with that freedom.»[2] The conditions which made it seem initially auspicious and productive for Buñuel to resume working in Spain for the first time in over twenty years have already been described elsewhere.[3] What is worth emphasising here, however, as Buñuel himself confesses in another interview, is that *Viridiana* exposes both his enduring interest and emotional involvement in Spain's chequered destiny, and also its self-conscious reformulations of thematic and stylistic trademarks associated with his earlier work. Before considering the more universal, timeless qualities that this film —in common with all the others, regardless of their country of origin— explores and develops, it is worthwhile trying to locate its relevance to the more specifically local social and political contexts of Spain in the 60s.

Buñuel's regular offscreen allusions to Spain and to its special place in his affections obviously lead one to suppose that like many other emigrés he must have been absorbed by the events of the immediate post-war period which had resulted in Spain's initial isolation followed by its recovery of respectability in the eyes of Western democracies. So in a film where the script is wholly original (written by Buñuel and Julio Alejandro), where there is not even the most rudimentary need to refer to the authority of a prior text (as is the case, of course, in *Tristana, Nazarín, Belle de Jour, Diary of a Chambermaid*, etc), Buñuel is free to give shape to his private

---

[1] See MAX AUB, *Conversaciones con Buñuel* (Madrid, 1985), p. 458.
[2] See *The World of Luis Buñuel*, edited by JOAN MELLEN (London, 1978), p. 216.
[3] See GWYNNE EDWARDS, *The Discreet Art of Luis Buñuel* (London, 1982), pp. 143-46.

fantasies and preoccupations with even less inhibition than usual and, as he remarks, the result was a film that in many respects both summarised and embroidered forms and themes that had regularly obsessed him. [4] But such freedom from the tyranny of other texts also meant that in *Viridiana* there could be veiled allusions to the ambivalent social reforms and ideals of the dictatorship. As has already been noted, *Viridiana* looks very much like a microcosm of Spanish society in the 60s: five levels of society are represented through the beggars, or the dispossessed; the peasantry (the labourers on the estate); the proletariat (the workers brought in by the estate's new owner, Jaime's illegitimate son); the church (the convent where Viridiana is a novice); and the landed gentry (Jaime, and eventually his son and Viridiana). [5] Beyond that one could say that Don Jaime himself, a role of multiple symbolic complexities, represents the diseased spirit of an antique Spain that had resurfaced under Francoism. Not, admittedly, a Falangist in the strictest military sense of the term, Don Jaime is nevertheless the moral, perhaps even the spiritual, harbinger of obscurantism in Spain's newest Dark Age. Aptly named Jaime, he is the «discreetly» monstrous «other» of Spain's patron saint, inwardly corrupt, lacklustre, haunted by memories, and presiding over a country —symbolised by the ramshackle, gloomy, cluttered-up estate— potentially great and productive, yet sadly almost doomed to oblivion. The irony of the allusion is that in consumer terms Spain in the late 50s and early 60s was beginning to enjoy unprecedented material prosperity. Nevertheless the undoubted benefits of such enviable economic achievements were hardly sufficient on their own to seduce Buñuel and other radical opponents of authoritarianism into accepting the concomitant darkness of censorship, patriarchalism, ultra-conservative morality and triumphalism.

This image of a Spain still toiling under the supervision of reactionaries of Church and State is therefore one that Buñuel could not possibly conceal. And so, on the one hand the pervasive influence of the more negative, restrictive side of religion in the affairs of the state is carefully and prominently located in the film's narrative structure: Viridiana's Mother Superior is a sinister woman, wearing Quevedesque spectacles on a face whose habitual expression suggests suspicion, curiosity and repression; and, on the other, the *guardias civiles* who, though making their entrance for the relatively trivial reason of informing Viridiana about the death of her uncle, nevertheless manage through their grouping and framing in the film's visual rhetoric to symbolise menace, recalling, through their presence, the sinister role of their counterparts in Lorca's *Romancero gitano*. Jaime himself, insofar as he is politicised allegorically, is a chip off the old Caudillo particularly in the

[4] See MELLEN, p. 18.
[5] See MARTI ROM, «*Viridiana:* vida y milagros», *Cinema 2002* (March 1978), pp. 68-73, p. 72.

extent to which, like some petty offshoot of Nietzsche's «Superman», he is eternally willing to subject others to his terrible will. The resemblances between Jaime and Franco are, of course, only very fleeting —the Caudillo can surely not even in his most idle moments have thought about his own suicide by hanging as a remedy for the nation's ills— and though one is certainly expected to note the political relevance of the film's situational complexities, there is quite clearly no attempt to construct an overtly allegorical framework. More pertinently, one could argue that *Viridiana* is an apt metaphorical crystallisation of Spain's 60s identity, formed largely out of the ideologically reactionary influence of centuries. A society that had largely ignored its rival traditions of liberalism is brilliantly reconstructed in its imaginative equivalent, the seedy world of *Viridiana,* in a film that constantly refers its audience to freer political and social *ambientes* only through evocations of their absence.

Yet if *Viridiana* is the desired fusion of Buñuel's recollections of Spain's pre-dictatorship past with angst-ridden images of its uncertain present, the film is also, very complicatedly, a meditation on Buñuel's own practice, an opportunity for returning to the historical and artistic roots that had continued to sustain him in Mexico. Beneath more elementary levels of significance *Viridiana* is very much a private, self-conscious text, a film full of Buñuelian intertextuality, at once illuminating and commenting on much previous work. Like Borges' stories, particularly «Pierre Menard», *Viridiana* is as informative about its past as it is about its present, and in its wide-ranging commentary on earlier preoccupations two issues are of primary significance: the unification of love and death, and the nature and function of art itself.

Among the clamour of voices speaking through *Viridiana,* two can very distinctly be heard, Buñuel's own *Abismos de pasión* (1953), and William Dieterle's *The Portrait of Jennie* (1948). These two films, notwithstanding all appearances to the contrary, are very closely related in Buñuel's imaginative development; they are almost doubles of each other, one, *Abismos,* dark, the other, *Portrait,* light, and each combining in various ways to prepare the ground for *Viridiana.* The fate of both films has been relatively similar: both have more or less sunk into oblivion, for while *Abismos* had initially been downgraded by Buñuel himself even though *Wuthering Heights* was a novel very dear to the hearts of the early Surrealists, *Portrait,* as Buñuel points out in his autobiography, *Mon Dernier Soupir* (1982), was misunderstood by almost everyone upon release and failed as miserably at the box office as in critical opinion. [6]

However, if one examines *Portrait* with the slightest degree of critical detachment one sees how very closely it resembles *Viridiana* in a multitude of different ways, and how influential it must therefore have been in its imaginative origins. The idea that Buñuel, a director of «art movies», should

---

[6] Luis Buñuel, *Mon Dernier Soupir* (Paris, 1982), p. 278.

however minimally be influenced by a «popular» Hollywood product might at first seem like a surprising, if not even a shocking proposition. But when one considers that other European art directors have been similarly inspired (e. g. Sirk over Fassbinder, etc.), and that many of the great Hollywood directors had themselves started their careers by making European art movies (Lang and others), Buñuel's susceptibility to parallel influences is not surprising. All of this is quite separate from the influence over the 1927 Generation (to which, particularly through connections with the Residencia and Lorca, Buñuel belonged) of Hollywood's silent cinema —especially the comic cinema— that Brian Morris has already very helpfully described.[7] In any case, Buñuel himself is not at all embarrassed by acknowledging his debts whether to European artists, like Lang, Dreyer, and Murnau, or to Hollywood directors like Dieterle.[8]

The plot of *Portrait* very simply is this: a luckless, though obviously talented, painter (Joseph Cotten) meets a young girl (Jennifer Jones) in Central Park only to discover that she must be a ghost. He continues to meet her periodically in New York, usually by chance, but sometimes by design, and on each occasion he is perplexed by her increasing maturity which advances far more dramatically than the time lapses between their meetings would realistically have allowed. At first he becomes fascinated and then obsessed by this gradually evolving young woman whose other-worldly face he begins to paint (the portrait of the title), and so overwhelmed does he become by his infatuation for someone he eventually discovers is in reality dead that anyone familiar with Buñuel's range of interests can immediately begin to see its background presence, even at this fairly banal level, in *Viridiana*. The connections between the two films start here, for *Liebestod*, the Death Instinct of Freud's late essay *Beyond the Pleasure Principle* on the conflict between life-preserving and death-dealing inner tendencies, is of course a major theme of many Buñuel films (e. g. *Belle de Jour, Le Charme discret de la bourgeoisie, Le Fantôme de la liberté*).[9] Consequently, before scrutinising more carefully the more elaborate connections between *Portrait* and *Viridiana* it would be appropriate to look a little more closely at the *Liebestod* theme in a film where Buñuel himself indulges his own fascination with it, *Abismos de pasión*.

In spite of Buñuel's frustrations and disappointments over *Abismos* there are a number of elements in the film which make it in our view comparable with some of his most powerful and most brilliant work.[10] The film is, first,

[7] BRIAN MORRIS, *This Loving Darkness* (Oxford, 1980).
[8] *Mon Dernier Soupir*, p. 277.
[9] See SIGMUND FREUD, «Beyond the Pleasure Principle», in *On Metapsychology. The Theory of Psychoanalysis. Beyond the Pleasure Principle. The Ego and the Id*, edited by JAMES STRACHEY (Harmondsworth, 1984).
[10] On *Abismos de pasión*, see AGUSTÍN SÁNCHEZ VIDAL, *Luis Buñuel. Obra cinematográfica* (Madrid, 1984), pp. 179-84.

evidence of the early Surrealist's ambivalent attraction to *amour fou*. Second, it is also a monument to Buñuel's general devotion to the Gothic, especially its English variants in the hands of writers like Matthew Lewis. As he himself confides, his love for the chilly sensations of northern culture can be partially attributed to what he sees as his own typically Latin's boredom with sultry climates. [11] The justification is characteristically Buñuelian in its epigrammatic, witty provocation, and though only limitedly useful as a universal observation, it is very revealing nonetheless as a comment on his own addiction to the art of the lugubrious, the spooky, and the sepulchral. Like William Wyler's film version of *Wuthering Heights* (1939), Buñuel's limits itself to the first half of the novel, the point at which Cathy dies. But where Wyler's film is a lyricisation of the *amour* in «amour fou», Buñuel's is far more interested in its *folly,* and, moreover, in the vampiric and satanic tendencies it releases. For instance, whenever Alejandro/Heathcliffe kisses Isabela —not really kissing Isabela, only the memory of Catalina on Isabela's face— it is not on the lips, but on the neck, like some modern Nosferatu. And when the camera eventually finds Alejandro on the night of Cathy's death, he is heard and seen violently cursing her and condemning her to hell in a scene where the darkness has so totally absorbed him that he has become a diabolical silhouette struggling against the howling wind on a night comparable in horror to the scene at Golgotha on that night of Christ's crucifixion. These unmistakably Gothic touches —applied both here and elsewhere in the film, particularly for indoor shots designed to expose the shadowy corruption of life at «Wuthering Heights» and at the Grange— simultaneously draw attention to Buñuel's offscreen homage to the cultural traditions of Matthew Lewis, Wagner and others, and also to the visual style of the masterpieces of the Expressionist cinema, film's own version of the Gothic, a genre Buñuel had himself frequently commented on both in reviews and in impromptu remarks. [12] The *chiaroscuro* style of *Abismos* perfectly suits its central *Liebestod* theme which, matching Dieterle's treatment of the same issues in *Portrait,* is expressed in a way that is inseparable from the film's fascination with perception. Alejandro is so obsessed by his love-object that, like Rojas' Calisto in the *Celestina,* every action he takes, every desire he has, is coloured by his fatal infatuation. Even when, for instance, in the film's brilliant climax, Alejandro turns his eye away from Cathy as she lies in the tomb he has desecrated, he sees not the person who is really there —Cathy's brother, Hindley— only Cathy's ghost. Significantly, the method of her brother's revenge for his endless humiliation at the hands of Alejandro is by shooting his loathed rival in the eye, an ironically fitting destiny for someone who in life had suffered from distorted vision.

[11] *Mon Dernier Soupir*, p. 271.
[12] See PETER EVANS, «The Discreet Charm of the Revolutionary», *The Guardian*, 5-6-82.

Like Eben's frantic desire to join Jennie in eternity, Alejandro's «quiero morir contigo» is more than simply a deranged man's outburst of rhetorical sentimentalism released at the very moment of his terrible recognition of the emotional chasm of a life ahead without her; it is also, beyond all the implications of Sadean necrophilia that the film also characteristically releases, a complicated revelation of an individual's desire for liberation from the prison of mortality, in Freud's terms, «the instinct to return to the inanimate state», to become through death immune from the mutabilities of life in a supra-lunary state of immanent being. [13] This is the yearning for paradise as expressed in the poetry of Fray Luis, or, alternatively, the regressive tendency Freud called the Death Instinct, a tendency he claims to have discovered even in Plato's description in *The Symposium* of the origins of life. [14] Once severed from their other halves, Plato's primeval humans eternally search for their unique double, and in the process yearn for a pre-cultural state of being, for an earlier Utopia of the self, and therefore for death.

The epigraph from Euripides chosen for *The Portrait of Jennie* is a succinct reformulation of this complex set of longings: «Who knoweth if to die / Be but to live ... / And that called life / by mortals / be but death?» The epigraph follows a voice-over which comments: «Since the beginning man has looked into the awesome realities of infinity and asked "What is space? What is life? and What is death?"» These sentiments are a prosaic but nonetheless effective refashioning of Fray Luis' «Quando será que pueda / libre de esta prisión volar al cielo / Felipe, y en la rueda / que huye más del suelo / contemplar la verdad pura sin velo?». In *Portrait* Eben's means of capturing the ineffable is through painting, while in *Abismos* Alejandro's perverse satanic longings are liberated through *amour fou,* and in *Viridiana* Don Jaime seeks eternity through his attempts to transform Viridiana into his dead wife, a process that bears all the hallmarks of the artist's transformation of the chaotic material of reality into the highly-wrought patterns of art.

There are abundant intertextual allusions to art in *Viridiana:* both to painting (the famous reference to Leonardo's *Last Supper,* and the two portraits hanging in the lounge of Don Jaime and his dead wife), and to music (the Hallelujah chorus from Handel's *Messiah,* and strains from Mozart). While the «religious» music links Jaime with eternity (besides being the background soundtrack it is played by Jaime himself on the harmonium), and underlies his own «immortal longings» by functioning as the comic equivalent of Fray Luis' music of the heavenly spheres (the «son divino» of Francisco Salinas), the paintings are both vignettes summarising the film's themes and also further indications of Buñuel's art of the self-conscious. His abiding interest in the mechanisms of perception reaches a point here

---

[13] «Beyond the Pleasure Principle», p. 311.
[14] «Beyond...», p. 331.

where he seems to be recalling Freud's notion of scopophilia, the theory which postulates that the desire to see is frequently inseparable from the urge for sexual knowledge. [15]

The twin desires of seeing and sexual curiosity are frequently linked together in the film. When, for instance, in the famous scene where the beggars —collected by Viridiana for the gratification of her naïve Christian principles— are frozen into the attitudes of Leonardo's *Last Supper*, Enedina (played by Lola Gaos) pretends to take their photograph with her sex. The camera as *coño* is more than just a typically Buñuelian way of seeking to *épater les bourgeois*. Much more significantly, while recalling Freud's suggestive analysis of scopophilia, the association simultaneously draws attention to Enedina's perspective on life, which is sketchily envisaged as sex-obsessed (she is also the character making love behind the blind man's back during the banquet). Viridiana, by contrast, at a superficial level sees everything through religion, Paco through commerce, and Jaime through neurotic obsessions with death.

Jaime's psychological constitution is highly complex, since he is at once disturbed by culture into fetishistically prizing virginity like Mathieu in *Cet Obscur Objet du désir,* to the point of derangement (not for an instant pausing to note the regressive or misogynistic implications of his obsession), and also determined to impose his own vision of reality —however myopic it may be— on everyone around him. As well as over-valuing virginity, Jaime is, like Rabour, for instance, in *The Diary of a Chambermaid,* a foot fetishist. At one point we see him putting on some of his dead wife's wedding garments and note that he seems particularly keen on wearing her shoes, totally mindless no doubt of Freud's explanation that foot fetishism «owes its preference as a fetish — or a part of it — to the circumstance that the inquisitive boy peered at the woman's genitals from below, from her legs up». [16]

When we see Jaime's reaction to his first sighting of the mature Viridiana —a niece he had known previously only as a child— we realise that he is a man imprisoned by memory. He is still obsessed by his dead wife to whom Viridiana bears a striking resemblance, as her portrait hanging in the lounge keeps on reminding us. What Jaime sees in Viridiana, what he has idealised not only in her but also, we infer, in her dead aunt, is her ethereal, mysterious grace and fragility. Like a child at a madonna's feet he had fetishised her —as his preoccupation with her wedding shoes reminds us— into the mother to whose womb —the seed-bed of his own «inorganic» condition of existence— his death instinct seeks constantly to restore him. As played by Silvia Pinal, Viridiana / Doña Elvira is an Ideal both at the

---

[15] «Beyond...», pp. 126-29.
[16] SIGMUND FREUD, *On Sexuality. Three essays on the Theory of Sexuality,* edited by JAMES STRACHEY (Harmondsworth, 1981), p. 354.

trivial level of Buñuel's declared taste for the Nordic (and in that sense she is an embodiment of the frail, vulnerable and childish heroine of much Gothic literature), and, at the more complicated level created by the demands of the film's thematic preoccupation, with death itself. [17] Whether she is dressed in the ghostly white habit of her Order or in the wedding gown that had belonged to her aunt, Viridiana is a pale, Gothic, deathly vision whose other-worldliness is made all the more pronounced by her blonde hair, her wan, colourless facial expression, and her large sad eyes that, like Jennie's in *The Portrait* (at a crucial stage in her life Jennie also lives in a convent), «seem to come from far away».

As we observe Jaime looking at Viridiana we are compelled to adopt an ambivalent attitude to his perversion: we note the absurdity of his delusion spared none of Buñuel's comic touches, but at the same time we recognise the universal power of such delusions kept alive by memory. As Eben observes in *Portrait*, «My memory was beginning to play tricks on me, I was seized by memories so urgent that they were more real to me than what was before me. Everything reminded me of Jennie.» So, like Eben, and like the nameless wanderer of Góngora's *Soledades* who had failed, so tightly gripped had been his mind by the memory of his own beloved, to appreciate and respond to the outstanding beauty of the bride he meets on his journey («Al galán novio el montañés presenta su forastero», etc.), Jaime looks at Viridiana but tries to remould her into his dead wife, wishes to marry her only so that, like Tristan who married a woman solely because she too bore the same name of his beloved Isolde, he can preserve the memory of his own wife and thus sustain his neuroses (see Plate 3). Memory here is not the creative source of images Buñuel discusses in the first chapter of his autobiography; [18] it is a much more negative faculty, a sign of stagnation, which in political terms, of course, it could only be: Jaime's memories are the weight of cultural tradition —like the pianos and donkeys and priests pulled by their victim in *Un chien andalou*— still oppressing Spanish society, with even greater authority under Francoism.

Buñuel's fascination with memory as a symbol of imprisonment is related to his complex interest in perception. The film is full of instances of voyeurism, or eavesdropping: Ramona spies on Viridiana as she undresses, her daughter Rita spies on Jaime as he attempts to seduce Viridiana once he has drugged her, the leading beggar is, crucially, a blind man, and so on. [19] Before her return, Jaime had been just as isolated in his *finca* as Viridiana in her convent. Like Nazarín he had attempted to blot out life itself, to become self-sufficient, to find salvation through solitude. Like Nazarín, too, he fails to realise that the consolations of solitude are not deprived of poten-

---

[17] See MOLLY HASKELL, *From Reverence to Rape* (New York, 1974), p. 104.
[18] *Mon Dernier Soupir*, pp. 9-12.
[19] EDWARDS, pp. 143-68.

tial dangers and temptations. In the very midst of Viridiana's pure world and Jaime's illusionistic retreat lie the symbols of their own ultimate destruction: when we first see Viridiana at the convent our attention is held, as it is in a crucial scene in *Tristana,* by the pillars of the courtyard, foregrounded not only in each film as a verbal/visual reminder of the film's «pillars of society», but also, since these are films obsessed with sexual neuroses of various kinds, as symbols of the sexual origins of widespread social malaise. The pillars are the unconscious erections of repressed sexual desire.

Viridiana's sexuality and her maternal instincts are, of course, sublimated into religion. When she unpacks her bag and takes out the crown of thorns, the nails and the cross, it is noticeable that she cradles the Crucifix in her arms as a mother would her baby. This process of transference also characterises Jaime's behaviour: by imposing the recollected images of his dead wife on Viridiana he allows us to perceive the tyranny underlying some aspects of patriarchal modes of perception.

Buñuel visually highlights Jaime's mental imprisonment on a number of occasions, and nowhere more crucially than when he is seen watching from a bedroom window the skipping game played below in the garden by Viridiana and Rita. In her capacity to evoke memories of his wife Viridiana arouses a mixture of responses in Jaime, all of which are Buñuel's heightened versions of what he takes to be patriarchal attitudes common to men entrenched in the dominant ideology of Latin culture: Viridiana therefore excites his metaphysical longing for death and the inorganic state, and more limitedly, his blatantly ideological assumptions about ideal womanhood as well. She inadvertently stimulates his rage and violence, something that à propos of violence towards women generally Adrienne Rich has termed «rapism», since he feels not only inclined to rape her but also, as he explains to Ramona, to hit her. [20] The causes for the impulses of violence she stirs in him are left deliberately obscure. They may be partially explained by his unconscious desire to trivialise or infantilise her, to strike her rather as an authoritarian parent might strike an irritating, disobedient child. Through the portrayal of Jaime one senses that Buñuel's interest in mature men's sexual tastes for waif-like, innocent young girl-children is not simply observation of deviant instinct, rather a way of questioning widespread ideological attitudes. *Belle de Jour* is another film where associations between women and children (Belle is defined by the Sadean M. Husson as a «collégienne précoce») are treated with some complexity. So here, as Jaime looks out, he sees Rita and Viridiana, two people whom his deadening gaze locks together in the imprisonment of social perception. During her absence Viridiana has already been prefigured in Rita, and now they are made to share each other's attributes: infantilized, controlled, desired as entirely submissive (that is what M. Hus-

---

[20] See ADRIENNE RICH, *Of Woman Born* (London, 1976).

69

son likes about the prostitutes at Mme Anais' — that they are «complète-
ment asservies»), powerless to resist total annihilation by the sexual, controlling, reductive gaze of the patriarch. But as he watches and transforms
their reality into the shapes created by his distorted perspective, so we see
him imprisoned by the window, Buñuel's visual symbol of Jaime's multiple
inner constraints and delusions. Though killed off half way through the
film, as surprisingly as Janet Leigh's Marion Crane was in *Psycho,* he is
arguably *Viridiana*'s real focus of interest, for though quite obviously the
film is interested at a narrative level in the story of Viridiana's journey
towards a certain kind of self-knowledge, he is the figure who continues
to control her life, even after death. The proof is the instalment, next to his
wife's, of Don Jaime's own portrait on the wall in the lounge.

The portrait is one of the film's many *mise en abîmes.* Like the competing
frames in, say, *Las Meninas,* the film's frames-within-frames accentuate Buñuel's interest in conflicting perspectives. So when the portrait of Don Jaime
takes its place beside his wife's one is quite clearly expected to see that
dead though he may be, Jaime continues to exert an influence on his surviving relatives, or, in the terms of the film's wider political perspective, that
the larger family of Spain itself is still governed by the patriarch whose
dependents remain confused by the contradictions of the dictatorship's revi-
talised medievalism. There is a superb irony in Jaime's suicide, for just as
in life he had been as if possessed by a dead woman, so now with Jaime
departed, but with his portrait symbolically very firmly placed in its cultur-
al/ideological context, Viridiana and her cousin are very much controlled
or haunted by a dead man. He is worshipped unconsciously: though some
of the more superficial attitudes are ignored and even modernised, the
primary values that are handed down to Viridiana and Jorge are inseparable
from Don Jaime and the old order. That quiet, enigmatic smirk on his lips
as he makes his will, leaving everything to his illegitimate son and niece,
seems to suggest that there is a private satisfaction derived from the knowledge
that he will not only now finally be able to join his wife in eternity, but
that he will have left his estate to two people who in highly complicated
ways are his golems. Viridiana has left the convent to help run the estate;
the meaning of that seems to be not that the Church's influence has been
shrugged off, but that with the Church still very much a part of her upbring-
ing and cultural background, only some of its more positive aspects like its
call to charity are from now on going to be ignored. The new Spain which
to a great extent Viridiana represents (the other part is symbolised by her
cousin) pays only lip service to Catholicism, avoiding its radical potential,
and concentrating instead on its instinct for repression.

5

STRESS ES TRES, TRES OR THREE INTO TWO WON'T GO

Though not reaching the highest levels of international recognition that Buñuel alone among Spanish film directors achieved, Carlos Saura (born Huesca, 1932), is unquestionably, after Buñuel, the director who has maintained a reputation abroad unequalled by any Spaniard since the 60s. Individual films by other directors — especially perhaps *El verdugo* (Berlanga, 1963), *El espíritu de la colmena* (Erice, 1973), and *Furtivos* (Borau, 1975) — have managed against all the odds of distribution and other difficulties to find acclaim beyond national boundaries. But while these films may have achieved a status that exceeds the reputations of their directors it is Saura's films that have regularly reminded international audiences of continuing vigorous film production in Spain. Working in the notoriously constrained circumstances of strict state censorship for so much of his career, Saura was nevertheless usually able, through techniques largely relying on allusion, metaphor and ellipsis, to make ambivalent films that were both innocent and subversive, radical and apolitical, in their treatment of issues which from one point of view were quite clearly related to the ideological and political consequences of dictatorship, but which from another could usually be read as private fantasies hardly threatening the stability of the regime.

With this double perspective in mind one could argue that although a film like *La caza* (1965) is, at its most profound thematic level, committed to an articulation of tensions associated with Nationalist ideology, it could also, at another level, be explained away as a relatively harmless narrative about idiosyncratic, slightly demented men who go hunting and end up by shooting not only rabbits but one another as well. *Ana y los lobos* (1972) too, seems from one point of view to be about the potentially disastrous effects of State-sponsored religion, while from another it could be understood as the victimization of a young woman by a family of grotesque caricatures in no way representative of typical oligarchies of the period. *El jardín de las delicias* (1970) and *Cría cuervos* (1975) are both in various respects crucially interested in interrogating Spain's recent past history, attempts through film to expose what Juan Tena has described as a period, following the Civil

War, which saw the «début de la manipulation et de l'escamotage du réel que vont subir, en particulier, les membres de cette "génération innocente"».[1] But they could all easily be dismissed as idiosyncratic, subjective indulgences. Admittedly *La prima Angélica* (1973) did cause something of a stir, but perhaps Saura's status as a director catering primarily for an international audience abroad and a minority audience at home spared him the harsher fate meted out to some of his contemporaries both in film (Bardem, for example) and in literature (Buero Vallejo, Alfonso Sastre, etc.).[2] In hindsight, of course, with the debacle of Francoism, it would be hard to deny that however private Saura's films were doubtless in some ways intended to be, their narrative and thematic motivations are irremovably grounded in the social and historical contexts of the time. The fantasies, neuroses, suffocations that so characterise the ethos and ambiance of the films cannot be seen purely in apolitical terms, delving as they do into the troubled regions of the contemporary and widespread malaise engendered by a repressive and archaic social system.

Despite its relative commercial and critical failure *Stress es tres, tres* is among Saura's films which seems to us most successfully and provocatively to merge these twinned attitudes of obsessive private and social introspection. Enrique Brasó's dismissal of the film is fairly representative of the sort of negative appraisal we are inclined to challenge: «*Stress* es posiblemente la película de Saura menos espontánea de su obra, menos "natural" y más forzada.»[3] Attacks of this kind seem centred on nebulous targets, and Saura himself, interviewed by Brasó in the same book, defends *Stress* by replying firstly, that in a film where he had greatest freedom and control he was deliberately trying to make a film about regressive adolescents:

> Yo presentaba a unos personajes adolescentes en su comportamiento sentimental... van efectuando una regresión, porque conforme va avanzando la película ellos se vuelven más niños, en una especie de búsqueda de extraño paraíso infantil en una playa en la que llegan a correr a cuatro patas.[4]

and, secondly, that such thematic preoccupations were coupled with a desire to detach himself from the more formal narrative constraints of his previous work, *Peppermint Frappé*:

---

[1] See JUAN TENA, «Carlos Saura et la mémoire du temps escamoté», in *Le Cinéma de Carlos Saura. Actes du Colloque sur le Cinéma de Carlos Saura*, 1-2 Fevrier 1983 (Bordeaux, 1983), pp. 11-29.
[2] For a probing analysis of the Spanish cinema and its struggles with censorship and other problems associated with audience reception, see JOHN HOPEWELL, *Out of the Past: Spanish Cinema after Franco* (London, 1986). We are grateful to the author for having shown us the typescript prior to publication.
[3] See ENRIQUE BRASÓ, *Carlos Saura* (Madrid, 1974), p. 189.
[4] See BRASÓ, p. 204.

> En *Stress* no se cuenta nada. Yo siempre he estado muy fascinado por esto
> de no contar nada. Un poco como *La caza,* que no tiene argumento porque el
> argumento será un poco ridículo contarlo... He estado siempre fascinado por
> la idea de hacer una película sin argumento. [5]

Reduced to its barest essentials *Stress* centres on three characters — a
married couple, Fernando and Teresa, and their friend, the *padrino* of
their *bodas,* Antonio — who take a weekend holiday together. They travel
by car to the seaside, where they intend to do some deep-sea fishing and look
at some land. On the road they have one or two adventures: they come
across a married couple who have been in an accident; they then stop off
at an aunt's house, where steadily developing tensions in the relationships
between all three become further intensified. When they reach their desti-
nation, the sea, Fernando imagines in a fantasy sequence that he harpoons
to death his friend Antonio, whom he suspects of adultery with Teresa. The
fantasy over, all three characters drive home together in the dark.

The film is inescapably peninsular in some respects, but it nevertheless
bears all the hallmarks of Saura's debts to other European film-makers,
especially Bergman, Godard and Buñuel. Like Bergman, Saura relishes cool,
cerebral dissections of the complex nuances of human behaviour; like Godard, he focusses on the socialisation of the self through language; like Buñuel, he implicitly argues that the roots of tyranny lie both in sexual repression and, especially in Spain, in the unnecessarily respectful status
given the Church and the Army. The film's violence, «medievalism», and
entomological symbolism are also very reminiscent of Buñuel.

As the characters drive through the barren landscape one is at once
reminded of the journey made by the professor, his relatives and the hitch-
hikers in Bergman's *Wild Strawberries.* Like *Stress, Wild Strawberries* is a
kind of «road movie», a journey into the hidden recesses of the self. In
Saura's film the journey takes in a route along the rocky shores of sexual
politics, particularly in so far as these are related to areas surrounding problems raised by marriage. In both films we are shown the true nature of
hollow men sheltering beneath masks of dignified or heroic masculinity, and
in this respect the film also recalls Godard's *Weekend.* Like the motorists
in *Weekend* hurtling towards barbarism, regressing towards infantile, irresponsible and primeval states of being, Saura's voyagers are themselves
becoming infantilized as they discourse with unrestrained banality on the
dawning apocalypse of civilization. All are characters whose «stress» is the
result of sexual paranoia conditioned by imagined or actual erosion both of
traditional notions of masculinity and conventional attitudes towards
marriage.

The idea of «stress» highlighted in the film's title originates, as Barbara Ehrenreich points out in *The Hearts of Men,* in the clinical work of

[5] See BRASÓ, p. 206.

Dr Hans Selye who in 1956 first used a term that was to become popularised in a subsequent book by Fred Kerner, *Stress and Your Heart* (1961).[6] It seems especially appropriate to relate Saura's notion of stress to American contexts of definition not only because of his refusal to translate the word into Spanish but also in the light of the specific reference in the film's voice-over to the USA as the world's epitome of consumerist values, the root ideological cause of the disease.

In the film's opening moments the voice-over associates stress more specifically with Julian Huxley, claiming that it is an «enfermedad de corazón... una aberración mental de úlceras», largely caused by «hastío... trabajo intenso... ritmo de la vida en las ciudades. Los ruidos... las preocupaciones». What Barbara Ehrenreich goes on to argue is that although «stress» is something primarily associated, as the voice-over asserts, with the pressures of urban life, it seems most particularly to strike at the male who strives in his role as breadwinner to comply with a stereotyped image of manhood, and to live up to the expectations of a society governed by predominantly conservative values:

> The most hazardous environment turned out to be the one that all men were expected to strive for — the home and office of the successful middle-class man. And the most vulnerable personality appeared to be the best adjusted, most responsible and clearly masculine.[7]

This «clearly masculine» personality has been defined as «Type A», driven by competitive urges, aggression, impatience, a man who considers that tranquillity, compassion, patience, flexibility are somehow either, at best, signs of inferiority, or, at worst, and judged by venerable standards of role divisions based on gender, ideals of femininity. In Saura's view, of course, such definitions of manhood do not simply prepare the ground for the institutionalised repression suffered by people in Spain following the Civil War. They are also potentially capable of creating in repressed societies everywhere else in the developed world the very conditions for the feared Armageddon of Nuclear War.[8]

Though the film's major focus of interest is primarily restricted to the psycho-sexual implications of postwar life in Spain, there are narrative and figurative features designed to draw attention to the apocalyptic consequences of world-wide repression. In this respect *Stress* sometimes has the generic look of a science-fiction film. Its bleak landscapes, dehumanised automaton characters, and documentary-style voice-overs combine in various ways to recall the narrative mechanisms of films like *Fahrenheit 451, Alpha-*

---

[6] See BARBARA EHRENREICH, *The Hearts of Men. American Dreams and the Flight from Commitment* (London, 1983), pp. 74-76.

[7] See EHRENREICH, p. 81.

[8] For the views of directors working in Spain under Franco see BBC TV's *Arena* programme, 2 December 1976

ville, and even, in its last sequence, *Kiss Me Deadly*. But while these apo-calyptic dimensions are, admittedly, kept in the background, invoked as the ultimate catastrophe to which inflexible adherence to such social systems will ultimately lead, the foreground of Saura's interest is the psycho-social processes from which stress is seen to emerge.

When Antonio remarks from his back seat in the car, very early on in the journey, that he has been reading a book about women who turned into men and vice versa, and when a little later on Teresa sardonically alludes to the Spanish proverb — visualised by Buñuel in *Tristana* — about women having to suffer «la pierna quebrada» (corrected by Antonio to «pata», a sign that he is well up on tradition), so that they can lead lives «encerradas en casa», we know that we are in the familiar thematic territory of sexual poli-tics, so characteristic of Saura's mature work. The paranoiac, voyeuristic jealousy felt by Fernando as he reacts to suspicions of Teresa's infidelity with Antonio allows Saura room for returning to questions concerning male and female expectations of selfhood that he had already tackled in such brilliantly evocative ways in films like *La caza* and *Peppermint Frappé*. While Juan Luis Gallardo and Fernando Cebrián provide the double per-spective for reflections on male aspects of the problem, Geraldine Chaplin brings her distinctive skill and persona to bear on questions related to women.

As Saura himself points out, Geraldine Chaplin's contribution to the film is indispensable:

> ... mi deseo era y es trabajar con ella, entre otras cosas porque se establece entre ella y yo una relación de trabajo muy intensa, y además de porque nos conocemos muy bien y porque ella es una actriz extraordinaria. [9]

Geraldine Chaplin is Saura's northern, pallid substitute for sultry Medi-terranean ideals of female beauty. She is his dark-haired Liv Ullmann. And just as Liv Ullmann, whom she resembles uncannily, could simultaneously express sensuality, otherwordliness and vulnerability in all her Bergman films, so in the clutch of films she made for Saura Geraldine Chaplin could vary the look of a woman drawn to sensual and intellectual challenges with the expression of someone who seems to be invariably victimized by life, especially by the tyranny of male presuppositions about the limits of woman-hood. The face, though striking, is not beautiful by conventional standards. In *Cría cuervos,* for instance, it serves to place in perspective the more social-ised image of beauty imposed on the other women in the film, characters whose destinies are limited to the frivolities of fashion and the indignities of adultery. There is a vivid freshness and innocence in Geraldine Chaplin's eyes and, about her lips, the faint trace of her father's «Charlot» expression,

[9] See Brasó, p. 198.

not only a touch of the great comedian's qualities as *eiron,* the scourge of hypocrisy and pretentiousness, but also a nervous, almost spectral, skeletal grimace around the mouth, particularly as she becomes animated either in conversation or in laughter. The lips stretch thinly over densely packed teeth that seem in their nakedness to suggest «desengaño» beneath the veneer of vitality they had formerly promised. The prominent cheekbones accentuate the skeletal contours, complementing the melancholy of her deep-set eyes, helping to create an eerie impression of *trompe-l'oeil.* The image is at once sensually vibrant and deathly pale, both a *carpe diem* and a call to love, what in Calderonian terms might be seen as the conflict from one of the great *autos* between La Hermosura and El Esqueleto. This duality of persona, both life-enhancing and death-dealing, is capable of almost infinitely subtle variations, and in their creative collaboration both Saura and Chaplin obviously strove to tease out the nuances of its dynamic potentialities throughout all the films they made together. In *Cría cuervos,* for instance, the emphasis of her part as Ana's mother, the role of the pure, innocent, unsophisticated and downtrodden wife of a man egocentrically seeking whorish qualities in his women, was more regularly on evoking images of vulnerability (a look contrasting very severely with the confident image projected in the same film by Chaplin as Ana, the grown-up daughter). In *Ana y los lobos,* on the other hand, her look projects the high-spiritedness in the role of the life-loving, girlish innocent abroad, ultimately victimized by men whose reason had become tainted by the vicious tendencies of a society founded on repression.

The flexibility of expression is highly suited to Saura's conceptual games based on the problematics of role-playing, and in *Stress* the joke is taken a stage further through his suppression of the information that Teresa/Chaplin, the usually «Dark Lady» of all her films, has in fact all along been wearing a blonde wig. Not until she removes it, along with most of her other clothes once they have arrived at the beach, do we realise that the image she portrays is even falser than we might have imagined. Like the fictional worlds created by Gracián —a writer to whom Saura pays homage in *Elisa vida mía*— Saura's contains very little that is stable, constant or reliable, governed as it is, like Gracián's by the mutable laws of a socialised reality. Among these, as the *Criticón* has it, are the vagaries of taste and fashion:

> Gran hechizo es el de la novedad, que como todo lo tenemos tan visto... lo que ayer fue un pasmo, hoy viene a ser desprecio, no porque haya perdido su perfección, sino de nuestra estimación... [10]

The laws of *novedad* in *Stress* are of course the characteristically 60s obsession with a dapper, almost anaemic kind of modishness. As Teresa

---

[10] See *El Criticón,* edited by P. ISMAEL QUILES, S. I. (Madrid, 1964), p. 24.

—in no senses here inheriting the spiritual or ethical qualities of her great namesake— parades around in perfectly shaped blonde wig, kaftan, or black bikini, she simultaneously satisfies her husband's cravings for *novedades,* frivolous and superficial tastes for the ephemeral, and arouses the latent violence and misogyny that these very cravings seem paradoxically to inspire.

Fernando's treatment of Teresa is almost a parody of male chauvinism, so extreme is its crudity. He patronises her by excluding her from various aspects of his conversation with Antonio en route to the aunt's house («eso no es cosa tuya»); by offering her flowers, conventional symbols here of patronisation, as a peace token following the adolescent caper of driving away for a while to leave her abandoned in the countryside with only Antonio, whom he hopes to provoke into Donjuanism, for company; by attempting to enjoy his conjugal rights at a moment when only boredom seems to motivate him; by forbidding her to keep the insect presented to her by Pablito; by expecting her to nurse his wound after the accident with his brother's motorcycle, following an incident deliberately aimed at putting her safety in danger; by ordering her to remove the black stocking she picks up on the beach, and which she wears as a provocative but ultimately harmless gesture during her mock fashion parade in front of Antonio; and by spanking her on her bottom across his knee while he intones, «que aprendas a obedecer. Esto es lo que les pasa a las niñas mal educadas como tú».

Though Saura's most profound interest in the subjugation of Teresa lies in his customary exposure of sexual tyranny, there is another, less complex element in his portrayal of her victimization that also deserves some attention. Through Teresa Saura glances as well at the superficialities, not to say puerilities, of high fashion. The 60s were, of course, a period that saw the previously unrivalled status of filmstars as icons of glamour begin to fade as other types of «star» began to compete for the recognition and acclaim of the star-crazy or fashion-conscious. Not only TV stars but perhaps for the first time too on such a grand scale models like Jean Shrimpton and Twiggy achieved the sort of universal fame that had previously been largely restricted to movie stars. Antonioni in *Blow Up* was one film director who had brilliantly caught the mood of the era in this respect; John Schlesinger in *Darling,* and to a certain extent, François Truffaut in *Fahrenheit 451,* were to use Julie Christie as an emblem of the hollowness at the heart of the international jet-setting fashion world. In *Stress,* but also in *Peppermint Frappé,* Geraldine Chaplin is asked to act out Saura's damning comment on the adolescent, empty attitudinising that this devotion to fashion had engendered. As Teresa pouts, poses and flaunts her body in a caricature of the 60s model's range of postures the soundtrack wavers between the lazy, empty cadences of a very evocative Bossa Nova from the period, and a rather crass, jolly, aimless melody given the format, tone and rhythm of a Swingles Singers number. Both the Bossa

Nova as a genre and the Swingles Singers as a group were highly popular in the 60s, and both seemed to epitomise the vulgar, bloodless quality of the chic style so admired in the period. As if that were not enough Saura compounds this image of puerility with dialogue that is very easily its match:

> ANTONIO: ¿Española?
> TERESA: Sí.
> ANTONIO: ¿Casada?
> TERESA: Sí.
> ANTONIO: ¿Con hijos?
> TERESA: Sí.
> ANTONIO: ¿Tiene algo en contra del rinoceronte?

Antonio and Teresa, not wholly anaesthetised by their ambiance, self-consciously comment on the inanities of dialogue associated with fashion events, TV programmes and publicity stunts desperately keen to create an atmosphere of clever banter eulogising the success of the consumer society while blandly ignoring the consequences of its availability for the landscape, the Third World, social structures in the developed world, not to mention its ideological preparations for the reality of nuclear war. As mature men and women with adolescent minds address themselves to the metaphysics of fashion —Gracián's *novedades*— the voice-over's earlier reminders of the less frivolous issues of life serve to create contrasts which make all the more horrific the insouciance and superficiality of characters cast as representatives of the ruling class.

While Fernando is almost wholly lost to the cause of bigotry and artificiality, Teresa is on occasion seen to be discreetly conscious of her predicament. Though guilty of immaturity herself, she sometimes seems to recognise that she and perhaps through shared experience women generally are the victims of patriarchal fictions condemning them to parts of limited range and significance in the social dramas of life. Like the author figure in *El gran teatro del mundo* (crucially alluded to in important scenes of *Elisa vida mía*), or like Basilio in *La vida es sueño*, Fernando, and through him patriarchy itself, dispenses the roles that everyone in his game of life will play. So when Teresa, particularly as she is wearing another woman's dress (Beatriz's kaftan), remarks, «Yo no soy un objeto», one feels that Saura intends her words to have a relevance beyond her own immediate circumstances to the plight of all women subjected to such indignities of status.

The film argues that it is precisely the unforeseen consequences of this sort of confinement of women to restrictive social roles — their identities understood primarily in terms of their relationship with men — that lie at the root of the most severe cases of male stress. Men are taught, as Barbara Ehrenreich argues, that real maturity lies in their growing up to become breadwinners, to renounce the life of immaturity associated with bachelorhood. [11] Growing up is synonymous with socialisation through marriage, the renunciation of the independent, adolescent life of the warrior, a theme repeatedly developed in American cinema, particularly the Western. The problems this sort of social education raises are that people embrace such concepts of maturity before having had the chance fully to explore their youth and adolescence, the time of adventure, risk and experimentation. So as the prematurely mature man begins to discover in marriage the realities of having been denied the opportunity of fulfilling himself properly in premarital experiences, he begins irrationally to blame his wife for his domestication. Women, following the rhetoric of the disenchanted male cheated by his own patriarchal legacy, exist only to trap men. Having no impulse other than to find husbands who will support them everlastingly, women —so the logic goes— are life's true predators. This mode of thought, so frequently cited by sociologists and feminists as an explanation for aggressive male behaviour towards women in marriage, is quite clearly used as an ingredient of male patterns of behaviour in Stress. Like Cervantes' curioso impertinente Fernando spies on his wife voyeuristically, actually invites his best friend to go on holiday with them (Teresa complains to Fernando that he has insisted on inviting Antonio to join them), and seems almost to go as far as to will him —like Lotario in the Cervantes story— to seduce Teresa so that, also rather like Buñuel's El, he can blame her for all his unhappiness and frustrations, manufacturing a situation that will vindicate his irrational violence and resentment towards her.

In some ways Antonio is Fernando's double; not in the Gothic sense of an evil «other», but more as a libidinous challenger of the social order, particularly of the expectations and conventions of marriage. While projecting an image of carefree bachelorhood Antonio is also a kind of perverted ideal for Fernando, the libidinous transgressor of pre-marital life, someone he can at once admire (since he restores more irresponsible, freer modes of being), and condemn (by the standards of what Freud calls the Superego, the social ideal constantly repressing anti-social desires). Forced to comply with social expectations which insist on marriage as the natural early goal for all decent men, Fernando is the mouthpiece of the confused male who discovers that his needs are not satisfied by the presence of a wife prepared to act out roles very much in keeping with what is expected of her under patriarchy (see Plate 4a). Fernando is the image of the male who yearns for the life of pre-marital independence from which, perhaps largely owing to social pressure, he had been untimely plucked, the kind of life that might have allowed him to release the dynamic, quasi-heroic tendencies he feels he can now seldom if ever indulge in marriage.

There are two climaxes in the film that very clearly illustrate Saura's convictions about the repressed, patriarchally-defined masculinity that erupts

---

[11] See EHRENREICH, pp. 11-13, 14-28, 29-41, 42-51, 169-82.

in ideologically conventional marriages. The first occurs when at the aunt's house Teresa has taken the horse, Lucero, out for a ride. As she gallops off into the countryside an image is created of a woman's temporary liberation from the suffocations of her traditional marriage. The unified rhythm of horse and rider suggests a world of nature, of rediscovered pre-civilized harmony. Realising that Teresa has set off on Lucero, Fernando follows her on his brother's brand-new motorcycle. Once he catches up with her he begins menacingly to ride around her. He accelerates, and in so doing begins to alarm the horse, who rears up. The brutality of the machine, its noise and energy, its unmistakably phallic metal rigidity, all combine to create an effect of masculine aggression roused against an act perceived by the conventional male as insubordination committed by a wife apparently showing too much independence of spirit. Saura here brilliantly captures that suffocating rage so characteristic of the conventional, undemocratic male desperately anxious to turn his mate into the scapegoat of his own perilous confusions of identity.

The second climax occurs when the trio of friends finally arrives at the beach. By now persuaded that his wife and best friend are adulterers— he has actually seem them kissing in the sea— Fernando imagines a scene where he is lying on the sand waiting for Antonio to emerge from the sea, eternal symbol here as elsewhere for the origins of life and of sexual desire. Antonio rises from the water as if dripping with the very elixir of erotic fulfilment, and Fernando's harpoon aims straight for his heart. This act follows his harpooning of a reproduction in a magazine of Gisbert's painting of the execution of Torrijos which, as we have already noted, is the most significant sub-text of *Si te dicen que caí,* by Juan Marsé. In his fantasy, switching now from magazine to the realm of his own perversely manufactured *ménage à trois,* Fernando pulls the trigger and finds his target. As he falls dying, to the accompaniment of Teresa's shrieks of horror, Antonio recalls through his posture the attitude adopted by the St Sebastian of Ribera's famous painting, a copy of which hangs in the aunt's house, where it had provided a crucial background image as a frame within a frame to some of the most important scenes in that setting.

In killing Antonio so cruelly in the fantasy, and not Teresa herself, Fernando succeeds nevertheless in assuring us that he aims to hurt her with maximum effect by forcing her to witness a scene that will remain etched horrifically on her mind for the rest of her life. Furthermore, he revitalises his manhood as a hunter and, in a perverted, sadistic way restores in sexual terms, as Anthony Storr puts it, *vis-à-vis* a general discussion of male sexuality and self-esteem, his damaged ego. [12] In becoming a hunter once more in the fantasy, Fernando is also now a perverted sort of leader, using violence to establish or re-affirm his authority in the family, the microcosm

---

[12] See ANTHONY STORR, *Human Aggression* (Harmondsworth, 1982), pp. 85-100.

of the state. He is less a version, in Ortega's schematization of heroic types, of the *hombre excelente* or *selecto,* destined to rise above the mass, and more an *hombre medio* perfidiously encouraged by dictatorship ideology to rise to the level of the *caudillo* himself by asserting the male's traditionally unchallengeable authority. [13] In killing Antonio, potentially the source of the family's threatened disintegration, Fernando acts out in his unconscious what Wilhelm Reich in *The Mass Psychology of Fascism* refers to as the «identification of the individual in the masses with the Fuhrer» (here, of course, Franco). [14] Furthermore, in envisaging the destruction of Antonio in religious terms, imaged as the martyrdom of St Sebastian, he succeeds also in exposing the contradictory tendencies towards self-assertion and self-denial, sadism and renunciation, that reveal the corrupt, tyrannical origins of the ideology to which he and his contemporaries are expected to succumb. Wilhelm Reich summarises the psychosexual implications of the authoritarian family like this:

> Sexual inhibition is the basis of the familial encapsulation of the individual as well as the basis of individual self-consciousness. One must give strict heed to the fact that metaphysical, individual and familial sentimental behaviour are only various aspects of one and the same basic process of sexual negation, whereas reality-oriented, nonmystical thinking moves along with a loose attitude towards the family and is at the very least indifferent to ascetic sexual ideology. What is important in this connection is that the tie to the authoritarian family is established by means of sexual inhibition; that it is the original biological tie of the child to the mother and also of the mother to the child that forms the barricade to sexual reality and leads to an indissoluble sexual fixation and to an incapacity to enter into other relations. [15]

But although in Fernando's limited imagination Antonio is the individual made to act out the role of St Sebastian, we know full well that he himself, much more than Antonio, is the real look-alike. He is the St Sebastian impaled on patriarchal ideals of masculinity, ideals that have both prompted him to cultivate violent, aggressive tendencies as evidence of his manliness, while simultaneously expecting him to become domesticated and socialised into the norms of a conventional marriage. More than a St Sebastian, Fernando, and perhaps eventually Antonio too, as well as most men brainwashed by what are ultimately fascist concepts of family life —given here a distinctive expression under Franco— are like the imprisoned *bichos* collected by Pablito, or the caged *hurones,* harmless rabbits and tormented beetles of *La caza,* dumb animals all, trapped and made to obey the whims of their masters, like the actors following the instructions of the Author in *El gran teatro del mundo,* or like the population of a whole country obeying the

[13] See *La rebelión de las masas* (Madrid, 1937).
[14] See WILHELM REICH, *The Mass Psychology of Fascism* (Harmondsworth, 1975), p. 97.
[15] See REICH, pp. 90-91.

dictates of its figurehead. The association between people and insects —with its ambivalently horrific and pathetic overtones— is brilliantly made both at the very beginning and at the end of the film. In the car the three weekenders all wear dark glasses, looking in close-up very much like the fly we later see, also in close-up, in Pablito's den, where he pins live bats to the wall. Like huge insects with monstrous, black, seemingly impenetrable eyes, these creatures wearing sunglasses recall the horrific associations of the great insect-horror films of the late 50s, *The Fly, The Return of the Fly* and *The Bat*. As the two men race on all fours at the beach, looking very much like outsize, grotesque insects, they are the dumb or adolescent, mindless yet pitiful creatures of a malignant society that has transformed them into monsters of human aggression, decadence and medievalism, nurtured on the consumerist and Nationalist values of phallic conquest, hierarchies and repression, so characteristic of the regime. [16]

[16] See also *Quarterly Review of Film Studies,* vol. 8, No. 2 (Spring 1983), edited by KATHERINE KOVACS, exclusively devoted to the Spanish Cinema of the post war period.

6

THE EUROPEANIZATION OF CARMEN

Freeing himself from the more crudely historical and political preoccupations of films like *La caza* (1965), *La prima Angélica* (1973), and *Cría cuervos* (1975), Carlos Saura nevertheless continues in *Carmen* (1983), to survey crucial aspects of the ideologies and shibboleths that have helped shape the politics and history of modern Spain. Even though the *mise-en-scène* in this film avoids the politically self-explanatory settings of contemporary militarism, hunting parties (the Caudillo's own special pastime), and other evocations of the Civil War, *Carmen* testifies to Saura's characteristic-cally muted radicalism as expressed in the films made in the Franco era by continuing to raise thorny questions about a nation's residually unhealthy social and psychological organisms.[1] Here while the narrative traces the search of a director/choreographer (played with gaunt, humourless athleticism by a handsome Antonio Gades) for the idealised embodiment of womanhood in an as yet undiscovered dancer who would play the lead in a Flamenco version of Bizet's *Carmen,* Saura's *intimista* style —though here abandoning the Bergmanesque aura of other films outlining the dynastic complexities of individual families— allows room for exposure of the wider, infinitely problematical family of Spain itself, still convalescing socially and psychically after decades of reactionary government.

Through Antonio's search for an ideal Carmen, Saura at once exposes an individual's private sexual neuroses and a nation's uncritical adherence to socially damaging stereotypes and clichés of role and gender (see Plate 4b). The film assumes almost mythic proportions as its thematic drive increasingly gains momentum from indirect allusions to the myth of Pygmalion, here transformed into Antonio, the show's director, implicitly aligning himself with the patriarchal figures of history and myth to create a dependent Galatea, imaged as a dancer plucked from obscurity to reflect on stage the narcissistic persona of her mentor. Carmen is remodelled in

---

[1] Erice's recently released *El Sur* is another film which can be read in this way. See our «Erice's *El Sur*: a Narrative of Star Cross'd Lovers», *Bulletin of Hispanic Studies,* LXIV, 3 (1987). 127-35.

the film's major setting, the rehearsal hall of mirrors where she reproduces his own notions of glamour and social value, and in so doing recalls Freud's views on the superior narcissism of the male, eternally seeking to perfect the objects of his gaze through imposition of self-centred ideals and attitudes.[2]

Saura's achievement in this film is to make one see that Antonio's life, fashioned by the contentious and divisive heritage of his own culture, is not wholly motivated by his own inner drives. At the crudest of historico-political levels one might argue that in mounting a production of *Carmen*, in searching for a particular Carmen, Antonio is a representation of post-dictatorship Spain's timely inward Odyssey, a quest for images and voices silenced and darkened by forty years of cultural and political repression. Yet, as it is, and given the particular form of his pursuit, Antonio is to a certain extent still unconsciously retarded by lingering Francoist intellectual and cultural assumptions which eventually lead to death, a fate which might have been avoided had the primary aim of the project been one of serious introspection after the wasted years of dictatorship. The stage death to which the Carmen of the drama must submit is mirrored by the offstage death that meets her impersonator a victim even after Franco as much of resilient ideological tyranny as of *amour fou*.[3]

Saura's characteristic taste for highly wrought forms of *mise en abîme*, rôle playing, theatricality —as much the legacy of Bergman (compare, for instance, *The Virgin Spring* and *Ana y los lobos,* or *Cries and Whispers* and *Cría cuervos*), as of Buñuel (comparisons too numerous to catalogue here)— is once again conspicuous in *Carmen* where onstage life reflects fictitious life offstage which in turn reflects —very complicatedly— real life offstage. The distinctively claustrophobic ambiance of the film, where the greater part of the action takes place in the rehearsal hall, cut off from everyday life, its huge window reflecting the real world outside, but also a barrier to its accessibility, helps create the sense of a social microcosm where the characters are simultaneously performers, audience, stage hands, etc. The borders of role definitions in this neo-Calderonian dream or fictional world are blurred to the point of indivisibility, and so indiscriminate and deliberately confused does this practice become that at one point it really is not clear where illusion ends and reality begins, as Antonio duels with Juan, Carmen's husband, at the end of a game of cards shortly after the latter's release from prison. Though the duel between Antonio and Juan

---

[2] See FREUD, «On Narcissism, an Introduction» (1914), in *Collected Papers* (London), Vol. IV, p. 30.

[3] In the first of her maudlin monologues in *Tiempo de silencio*, Dorita's grandmother mistakenly calls Dora, her daughter, «Carmencita», a detail which Juan Tena interprets as indicating an authorial intention to debase the archetype of «la Carmen de España». See TENA, «Pour une lecture de *Tiempo de silencio*», in *Luis Martín Santos: Tiempo de silencio* (Montpellier, 1980), p. 72.

naturally touches on complex psychological and aesthetic issues, part of the effect of Juan's involvement at this point is to highlight the film's social dimensions. The film's projected interrelationships of art and life are presented ambivalently, both passionately and claustrophobically. No *On The Town* (1949) this, a set-free exploration of the sights and sounds of a vibrant, «open city», more a tragic *Kiss Me Kate* (1953), its set-bound restrictions functioning as an apt image for a nation's dead-end socialised *creencias*.

Though conscious of the existence of Juan, seen first in jail, in one of the film's many images of imprisonment, Antonio is prevented from meeting him until quite late on in the film when, having been set free and accompanied by Carmen, he arrives in time to see a rehearsal of the show. Antonio is himself seen reacting to his first sighting of Juan as the camera adopts a position outside the rehearsal building and catches him framed by the outsize glass window normally seen in the background, from the interior. The glass itself —traditionally a symbol of two-dimensionality, fragility and transparency— and its reflected images of the leafless branches of the trees surrounding the building, suggest the presence of an emotionally vulnerable man, entangled by the skeletal, ultimately fatal involvements of a natural passion only very recently consummated and whose premonitions of danger are clearly well founded in the vision of his feared rival.

Yet, in fact, Juan is not his most serious rival, only the first to expose his outmoded but nonetheless powerful and tormenting attitudes to love. Juan's presence serves to draw attention more assertively to the inner being of the lover whose deep-seated machoism is masked by superficially appealing romantic tendencies. Naturally enough, and in due course, the two men quarrel over Carmen. The excuse for their duel is a game of cards, and as they rise from the game following Antonio's accusations of foul play which have been stoked by Carmen herself in a gesture which seems mischievously designed to stir up trouble, the tensions and expectations of conformists in love are exquisitely stylised into the ritual of a Flamenco ballet duel played out in lighting conditions which throw huge dwarfing shadows on a sepulchrally bare background. As the two men thrust, parry and counter-thrust with long, unmistakably phallic sticks, their shadows construct images of the *Doppelgängers* of fatal desire. The clashing phallic sticks, the machine-gun fire of the duellists' heels as they go into their fiery dance, the shadows of death on the wall, all sustain the film's recognition of the dereliction as well as of the allure of possessive, patriarchally socialised modes of love. While we may feel that Carmen herself is far from ready for the more extremely confused and feminized man of post-feminist Europe, she is at least modern enough to know that pre-80s unregenerately authoritarian and possessive men are equally foreign to her taste. To a limited degree a representation of the new woman, whose voice had grown louder in the more radical areas of the dictatorship in the late sixties —a period in Spain not entirely unaffected by world-wide movements towards alternative, disaffiliated systems of living— Carmen demands equal rights above all in determining with whom and on which terms she is prepared to share her body. She is Saura's antidote to centuries of addiction to the submissiveness and servility frequently demanded of women in Spain, something he had repeatedly examined throughout his film career.[4]

But the issues are never downgraded to caricature, as they were sometimes wont to be in films like *Ana y los lobos* —with its course-grained picture of military, religious and Oedipal bigotry and folly in the shapes of the three representative brothers— or *La prima Angélica* —and its Nationalist with the paralyzed fascist-saluting arm— for here one feels that Saura is at last able, his country now rid of a reactionary regime, to admit that tradition is not wholly cancerous, modernity not entirely Utopian. As the voices of past and present struggle to be heard it becomes clear that while Orpheus-like Antonio looks back, Carmen, in some ways the spirit of the new democracy, looks ahead. While the deafening sounds of the castanets at the dancing teacher's school serve partially to create an image of the survival of an all-engulfing ethos, Carmen herself rises above such traditional contexts to inflect these sounds with an avidly expected modernity. In her playing of the role with such grace and fire Laura del Sol has not found it difficult, as she herself relates in a recent interview, to earn the approval of European feminists:

> Las mujeres alemanas después de ver *Carmen* se quedaron alucinadas, las feministas se quedaron encantadas porque veían a una mujer fuerte, que dominaba al hombre. Fue una cosa impresionante.[5]

By contrast Antonio, the master of the revels, is an outwardly benign form of Spain's trust in tradition. In his search for Carmen one can see not only a man's desire for a serviceable woman but also an element of what could be called Saura's 80s rekindling of the spirit of 1898. With the collapse of the dictatorship, a new order upheld by a vigorous leadership —Juan Carlos and, initially, Suárez, and subsequently González— seeks to reaffirm Spain's rightful commitment to a European ideal, ultimately to be fulfilled with entry into the EEC. So, Antonio, in some very limited respects an amalgam of the king and his democratically-elected prime ministers, attempts to Europeanise a native, local culture: the European strains of Bizet are imposed on Andalusian Flamenco rhythms; early in the film there is a marvellously evocative moment where the guitarrists, led by Paco Lucía, follow their usual rhythms and then gradually try to adapt their chords, beat and harmonies to the more voluptuous sounds of the Bizet score booming through the amplifiers on stage but, in the end, symbolically prefer the native

---

[4] See PETER W. EVANS, «*Cría cuervos* and the Daughters of Fascism», *Vida Hispánica*, XXXIII, No. 2 (Spring, 1984), 17-22.

[5] See *Fotogramas* (September 1984), p. 20.

forms. These musical instances repeat the pattern already created visually where the allusions to Mérimée and Bizet are made while the credit titles appear over nineteenth-century prints depicting scenes from the novel/opera.

Yet even though Europeanization, which these sequences suggest, has a positive side, the rediscovery of a self beyond the Pyrenees simultaneously revives, more negatively, cliché and stereotype, for Bizet means not merely Europe but also the nineteenth century and all its regressive attitudes, just as Andalusia, Flamenco and Sevillanas are not just colour, form, passion and vitality, but a reductive, short-hand, touristic metonymy for the infinitely complex association of regions conveniently and loosely termed Spain. The limitations of Antonio's *Carmen* project are the shortcomings of an ideology's plaything.

In the variegated shapes formed by ideological constructions of the male self Donjuanism is an incontestably prominent feature, so it is not unexpected that in *Carmen* there is a poster, placed on a wall near the dressing rooms, announcing a Don Juan production — film or play is not quite clear — reminding everyone of cultural affirmation of virility. Like Zorrilla's Don Juan Antonio craves romantic regeneration through a deadly ideal; like Tirso's satanic precursor Antonio embodies a vision of the unyielding macho whose pulse is quickened by the chase. Though there is a suggestion that Antonio has not hitherto abstained from casting-couch protocol, the film is keen to freeze-frame only one exploit, to scrutinise his conduct during only one attempted victimization in order not only to expose the superficiality of his *courtoisie* (further underlined by his suggestion to Carmen that she read Mérimée's text, another of the film's images of authority), but also to show that owing to the changed circumstances of history and politics the biter is on this occasion well and truly bit. The stages of his attempted victimization are carefully created by Saura.

In a film meticulously and deliberately stacked with clichés it seems more than usually appropriate for Carmen to be described —following the idiom— as wolf-like. Her subjugation a fact of culture, in which language itself circumscribes her very being, Carmen and through her all women whose physical presence arouses indiscriminate sexual instincts incompatible with the deference due to virginal brides or respectful matriarchs, is constructed in Antonio's mind's eye as rapacious nature personified, a ferocious beauty whose conquest is likely to be all the sweeter for its thrillingly arduous challenges. The wolfish associations are given precisely the same degree of equivocation as may be found in Angela Carter's *Company of Wolves*, or for that matter, José Luis Borau's *Furtivos*, in all three of which sensuality is associated with darkness (Carmen, naturally, is dark like the self-consciously sexual woman of literary tradition) and wildness (she wears fur at one point, emphasising very clearly her sexual presence). As, full of mystery and self-conscious eroticism, Carmen fixes her gaze through her «ojos de lobo» on Antonio, she becomes only the latest example in a long tradition of women flattered by men into the straitjackets of literary hallucinations, a point carefully made by Saura yet apparently ignored by the reviewer Jorge Berlanga in this nevertheless pertinent recent observation:

> De la famosa Carmen conserva sobre todo esa mirada desarmante, que mide a su interlocutor de arriba a abajo, haciéndole sentir como un meque-trefe. [6]

Wolf, Spider Woman, Tiger Lady, Femme Fatale, Vagina Dentata, Witch, or quite simply, Carmen: these are the roles imposed on women free to release and indulge sexual instinct for the price of a vampish reputation. But in the promised Utopia of democracy, Carmen takes her sexuality for granted, scorns Antonio's outdated strictures, and seeks liberation from the past's authoritarian and controlling perceptions, not in the slightest inclined to deny her selfconscious eroticism.

Antonio's strictures, eventually articulated upon discovery of Carmen's dallying in the dressing room with a fellow-dancer significantly named «Tau-ro», are signalled much earlier through the film's mirror imagery which exposes Saura's double concern with self-knowledge and voyeurism. Films like *Peppermint Frappé* (1967) and *Cría cuervos*, with their obsessive portrayal of characters constructing self-definitions through collages cut out of fashion magazines, had already indicated a serious concern in social formu-lations of individual identity. Here in this room of eternal rehearsals a finished production, what would have been the symbolic agreement for a fixed set of post-dictatorship definitions and resolutions about self and society, is predictably never achieved. Saura creates a vortex of swirling but ultimately doomed proposals. These devotees of the dance, dedicating themselves to the perfection of balance, poise, rhythm and energy, reveal that the extreme aestheticism of their calling is nevertheless grounded in moral purpose. Like Ortega's ideal hunters, preparing themselves with austere, almost monastic powers of concentration for the ritual slaughter, Saura's dancers, like pro-fessional sportsmen and women too, have gone past the point of mere recrea-tion. [7] Gestures of limbs, leaps, flights, facial and bodily grimaces are all in strange but powerful ways tendencies and achievements of character. Constantly evaluating such achievement is the prominently enthroned danc-ers' mirror, here less the innocent monitor of individual development and more the obedient instrument of a voyeuristic director, who resolutely shapes the images projected through his selective, ideologically-distorted mind. For Antonio is also the eye of a social law; his role in the dance —as participant as opposed to director of the production— is not that of the transgressor

---

[6] See *Fotogramas* (September 1984), p. 17. On fur and fetishism, see SIGMUND FREUD, *On Sexuality, Three Essays on the Theory of Sexuality,* edited by James Strachey (Harmondsworth, 1981).

[7] See JOSÉ ORTEGA Y GASSET, *La caza y los toros* (Madrid, 1960).

Escamillo, the bullfighting symbol of inflexible virility. He is on the contrary a version of the Law's guardian, Don José, the upright social conformist, prey in the terms formulated by ideology to the caprice and will of sexually assertive women. Like Wim Wenders' broken hero in *Paris, Texas* he can visualise from behind the two-way mirror the woman of his fantasies. Like him too he comes to realise, though far more dimly, the corrupt powers that help give it form. What he surely fails to recognise is that he is the film's socially-constructed Father-figure, Carmen his longed-for seductive daughter.[8] Older than Carmen, he is, as has already been argued, the Pygmalion to her Galatea, still attached to the past (so he uses the older prima ballerina to teach Carmen the old ways), and constantly used by Saura as a symbol of traditional male demands upon women, here summarized as the infantilization of a cherished, but reified sexual partner. The social dimensions of the Oedipal drama merge with other preoccupations and as we watch we are compelled to note the tragic consequences of the over-valuation of virility. On one level the father-figure of the dance generates indisputable harmonies —the grace and form of the ballet— on the other he fails to renounce the culture through which he feels justified in indulging his uncontrollable violence. Outraged by what he sees as the humiliation of being forced by Carmen to share her love with other partners, he achieves the Pyrrhic victory of her death. Given the opportunity to use the ballet —in his capacity not as a dancer, but a director now— as a kind of autobiographical moment of truth (the association between bullfight and autobiography or self-analysis is brilliantly made by Michel Leiris in *Manhood*), to avoid merely celebrating, as Leiris puts it, «the vain grace of a ballerina», Antonio seems actually set on achieving through his direction of Carmen what Freud called the passage of a woman «from her masculine phase to the feminine one to which she is destined».[9] Carmen's response is precisely to resist this process in the changed political and historical environment which now allows her to do so. She refuses to be merely the object, preferring instead to be the agent of desire, no longer content to find a self-definition in the perspective of male necessity.

So, self-confident and conscious of the rising challenge to the traditional ethos, she is even able to risk herself in parody. After a mock-bullfight expressing in comic terms the place of machoism in the nation's psyche, staged as part of the birthday celebrations for a member of the company, Carmen walks on dressed in the marvellously camp *típico* «Sevillan» costume of cheap picture postcards: mantilla, multi-layered dress, exaggerated facial cosmetics, and fan.[10] This *grand guignol* spectacle of excess comically

---

[8] See FREUD, *New Introductory Lectures on Psychoanalysis*, vol. xxii (London, 1953-74).

[9] See MICHEL LEIRIS, *Manhood* (London, 1968), and FREUD.

[10] Compare LUIS BERLANGA's very recent *La vaquilla* (1985) in which a soldier *torero* betrays conventional expectations of heroism, and in general the *fiesta nacional*

89

restates the dominant culture's assertion that a woman's appearance is her identity. By the end of the film we will have learnt that «femininity» is no biological necessity in women, merely the socially-engendered persona frequently imposed upon them. The sight of this visual parody serves the additional purpose of enriching the film's theatrical metaphor: playing a *femme fatale* on stage, she now acts out in life the very fantasy that sustains the patriarchal images of the woman fashioned by culture, attractive, desired, but feared and, therefore, liable to punishment. Carmen self-consciously acts out an image of what has often been no less than a woman's destiny, the trap of the body, of fantasised sexuality, the alluring yet impure sexual transgressor of tradition. As she saunters into the convivial atmosphere of the party, the assertiveness of the modern woman shines through the tacky stereotyped exterior of her flaunted persona.

Yet Saura's observations of social and psychological complexities refuse to be satisfied with purely negative perspectives. Though to a limited extent Antonio is the embodiment of patriarchal commitment to the view of women as property, there are other respects in which his attitude to Carmen complicatedly raises questions about whether human unhappiness can have more than purely ideological causes. All too human questions arising from the insecurities of age, temperament and so on cannot be wholly understood in purely ideological terms. There is no denying that Saura is deeply interested in exposing through various aspects of Antonio's role in the film the infrastructure of sexual politics so rigorously defined in feminist debates of the last twenty years or so. For as well as being a creator his hero is also a director of women, both on and off stage, finding support for his sexual and social attitudes in the traditional associations of men with power, vigour, energy, intellect and control. Moreover, as Adrienne Rich, Juliet Mitchell and others have been pointing out, this power, where it is channeled into the creative energies of culture, can in some senses be understood as compensation for the creativity of motherhood. [11] Though quite obviously defined as an anti-mother, Carmen nevertheless still clearly retains the potentiality of motherhood which the male is unconsciously liable to envy. It is clear that as Antonio directs Carmen an underlying ambivalence —part desire, part misogyny— motivates his whole attitude towards her: by turns tormenting her, like some Von Stroheim of the dance, for the erotic longings her presence excites in him, by turns praising her for her implementation of his whims and fancies, he creates a performance that simultaneously represents the targets of his inwardly competing vilification and desire.

is exploited as a source of farce. In the complementary portrayal of *maja* and *torero* Saura ruthlessly demystifies male and female archetypes of Spanish culture, after LUIS MARTÍN SANTOS' radical analysis in *Tiempo de silencio*, pp. 182-83.
[11] See ADRIENNE RICH, *Of Woman Born* (London, 1976), JULIET MITCHELL, *Psychoanalysis and Feminism* (London, 1974), and, crucially, KATE MILLETT, *Sexual Politics* (London, 1971).

But Antonio's anxieties and failures arise as much from his own natural and circumstantial limitations as from ideological affiliations, and these are surely also responsible for his failure or refusal to recognise his own predominantly unconscious imposition of ideological stereotypes on Carmen. Expecting her to be the stereotyped mixture of what Freud understood as a woman's typical traits of psychology —narcissism, masochism and passivity— he finds instead the spectacle of a woman's emergence from these socially-conditioned ideological constraints, using her native intelligence, glamour and self-confidence to assert her own independence in the quest for her self-controlled destiny. He has not been taught to see that in Carmen's offstage rehearsals of the usual roles and practice a healthier social climate is being created: he is merely bewildered when he takes stock of the fact that it is she who leaves her lover's bed, she who tells her lover to control himself, she who commands him to dance for her private gratification, she who picks and chooses other sexual partners. (It is no accident that when the camera pans at one point to include scenes of offstage life during rehearsals it should reveal that the production's dressmaker in the new society is a man) Supported by the revived democracy's reforms in divorce laws, contraception, though not as yet abortion, the new woman disorientates a man not yet alerted to his own need to review possibly outdated notions of self and others. [12]

Like the strong male director or partner in the dance of countless Hollywood musicals, which in some ways this film resembles and lyricises (there is, for instance, a nice touch where Otto Preminger's *Carmen Jones* (1954) is visually quoted through Saura's dressing of Carmen for her first appearance in the film in orange and black, Dorothy Daindridge's costume colours for her first appearance in *Carmen Jones*), Antonio exerts power over his prima ballerina on stage. But there the comparison ends. Offstage, Carmen's natural and officially but perhaps not privately sanctioned assertiveness and independence are released from the formal artistic constraints in which her American predecessors — Ginger Rogers, Eleanor Powell, Ruby Keeler and others — had been frequently imprisoned. The thunderous din of the dancers' heels on the wooden floor, the ankle-high restive tracking shots up and down the *fondo* of the stage, and the stylised violence and controlled eroticism of the performers' physical contortions are not merely further examples of art's safely cathartic indulgences; they are vibrantly reformulated and acknowledged in women like Carmen who are no longer afraid in changing circumstances to rescue the radical potential of all art as ways of asserting

[12] In a controversial and closely contested decision made public on 17 April 1985, the *Tribunal Constitucional* ruled that a bill on abortion proposed by Felipe González's Socialist government and already approved by the Spanish parliament was unconstitutional. This event put into perspective that same government's achievements in legislating on divorce and contraception during its period of office beginning on 1 December 1982.

the demands and rights of women and men in life. To men unprepared for such radical reorientation Carmen's wilful assertiveness leads only to arousal of the venerable spectres of outraged virility. Unable for a variety of reasons to escape from the spiral of primarily ideological confusions surrounding the self, Antonio finally acts out the cliché that is the logical outcome of his growing anachronism of a life. Once he is finally rejected by Carmen on the grounds of his irremediable puerility he betrays the positive drives of the art he helps to create, and he ultimately kills, like Wilde's nameless lover, the very thing he loves. In the symbolic idiom of the film a country's search for sexual, psychological and political reconciliation is thus tragically thwarted. Carmen, symbolically one element of the new Spain's drive towards sexual equality, is killed by the surviving tendencies of the old order. Saura makes us feel though that even if she must die others will ultimately triumph.[13]

[13] Since writing this chapter we have had the opportunity to see an, as yet unpublished, article by DEBORAH HILL, «From Dictatorship to Democracy: Carlos Saura's *Carmen*», which borders on some of the territory covered here. Although we are in agreement over a number of issues raised by the film, we are not in sympathy with her view that the film shows Spain's trouble-free transition from dictatorship to democracy.

CONCLUSION

So as Spain began in 1936 to close its frontiers to political and cultural developments sweeping across Europe —recalling in so doing the efforts of the Counter-Reformers in the mid-sixteenth century— it was inevitable that its most gifted creative talents should rely, in their struggle to find appropriate forms for the nation's growing frustrations and blighted aspirations, on a shared stock of bleak images and disturbing, even if usually allegorical, narrative mechanisms. Consequently, while we have been anxious to define the distinctiveness of individual voices, we have been equally careful, taking our cue from Barthes and subsequent «deconstructionists», to respond to the collective voice which sometimes acquiesced in, but more frequently challenged, the stifling *creencias* of the Franco dictatorship.

All the texts discussed are characterised by over-arching images of disease or madness of one kind or another, something readable primarily in terms of a whole nation's social and moral decay. The cancers of *Tiempo de silencio,* the viscerality of *Dos días de setiembre,* and the fetishism of *Viridiana* are all, perhaps inevitably, the aesthetic formulations —as vividly visualised on the printed page as on the screen— of novelists and film-makers fed on the triumphalist fodder of social and psychological repression. Moreover, the shared reliance on paintings as *recursos* (Ribera's St Sebastian, the Torrijos picture, etc.), and the dependence on the familiar tableaux of Judaeo-Christian or pagan mythology (Cain and Abel, Pygmalion, etc.), are devices that reach beyond superficialities of convention to levels associated with the radical project of an intertextuality, where the problem of a heterogeneity of perspectives frequently becomes itself the true subject of the text. Yes, as Brian Morris points out *vis-à-vis* the literary and film genres of the 20s and 30s, one should note and carefully describe an obvious interaction of forms in the genres of the 60s, 70s and 80s, but in our view the eye imagery, *mise en abîmes,* film quotations, etc., of these later texts are to such an extent a recurrent feature of their frames of intelligibility precisely because the Spanish artist of the post-war years becomes conscious of the assault on authenticity by the insidious canker of a patronising ideology.

Like the retarded neurotics of Freud's case analyses (is Luis Martín Santos' Dorita a playful reincarnation of Freud's Dora?), the Don Jaimes and the Conrados of these texts are the zombies of an all-powerful system of values that has left them too traumatically socialised to trust either in the rational processes of their own minds, or in the ideals of a pre-«civilized» —and, on this reading, pre-Francoist— «polymorphous perversity» in which, as Marcuse and others argue, the sources of liberation and happiness truly lie. Rooted in historical realities, nurtured on the more infantilizing tendencies of patriotism, religion and phallocentrism, even those who have physically survived the Franco years are sometimes incapable —like Antonio in *Carmen*— of casting off the social and moral habits of an age.

By the time of *Carmen*, of course, the allegorical devices of texts born at the height of Francoism are replaced by less politically-motivated metaphors. Not that Saura and others are politically naive enough to believe that the new democracy immediately ushered in Utopia, but that with the larger political issues apparently settled, artists could once again make their primary focus areas of greater intimacy —without necessarily returning to the more «dehumanizing» corners of a modernist tradition— and, equally, begin the task of interrogating the legacy of the dictatorship, particularly in the field of sexual politics.

The fetishization of women, especially, either as spectacle or as domestic drudge —something that had already attracted the attention of, for instance, Buñuel and Marsé— becomes increasingly, with the rise of feminism in Europe in the 70s and 80s, a topic to which novel and film in Spain would turn with inescapable regularity. As the nation strives once more to restore its European heritage, it struggles through its art forms to demonstrate how enduring are the scars of ideology. And as Spain resumes its rightful place in the European community —in the broadest sense of the term— perhaps the time has also come again for its art —the art, for instance, of Luis Martín Santos, Caballero Bonald, Juan Marsé, Luis Buñuel and Carlos Saura— to be given the wider acclaim it undoubtedly deserves.

PLATE 1.—*El fusilamiento del general Torrijos y sus compañeros*, by Antonio Gisbert. Reproduced with the kind permission of the Museo del Prado, Madrid.

PLATE 2.—*Escena de brujas,* by Francisco de Goya. Reproduced with the kind permission of the Museo Lázaro Galdiano, Madrid.

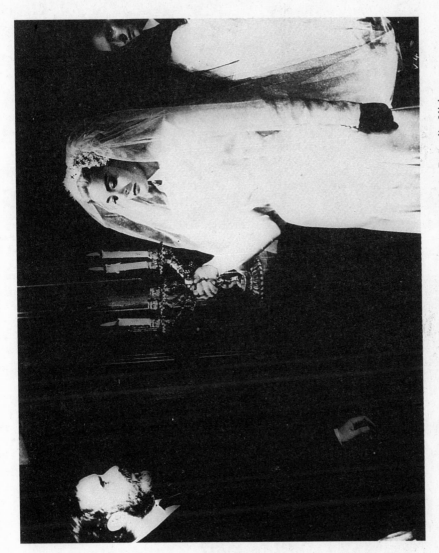

PLATE 3.—Don Jaime (Fernando Rey) and Viridiana (Silvia Pinal) in Buñuel's *Viridiana*. Reproduced with the kind permission of Contemporary Films Limited.

PLATE 4a.—Teresa (Geraldine Chaplin) and Fernando (Fernando Cebrián), in *Stress es tres, tres*. Reproduced with the kind permission of Elías Querejeta Productions.

PLATE 4b.—Antonio (Antonio Gades) and Carmen (Laura del Sol) in Saura's *Carmen*. Reproduced with the kind permission of Curzon Film Distributors Limited.